HOW TO MANAGE PEOPLE AT WORK

MANAGE PEOPLE
AT WORK

A Practical Guide to Effective Leadership

John Humphries

Second Edition

How To Books

By same author
How to Manage a Sales Team
How to Counsel People at Work

British Library cataloguing-in-publication data
A catalogue record for this book is available from the British Library.

© 1992 and 1995 by John Humphries

Published by How To Books Ltd, Plymbridge House, Estover Road,
Plymouth PL6 7PZ, United Kingdom. Tel: Plymouth (01752) 735251/
695745. Fax: (01752) 695699. Telex: 45635.

First published in 1992
Second edition (revised and updated) 1995

Note: The material contained in this book is set out in good faith for
general guidance and no liability can be accepted for loss or expense
incurred as a result of relying in particular circumstances on statements
made in the book. The laws and regulations are complex and liable to
change, and readers should check the current position with the relevant
authorities before making personal arrangements.

Typeset by PDQ Typesetting, Stoke-on-Trent, Staffs.
Printed and bound by The Cromwell Press, Broughton Gifford, Melksham,
Wiltshire.

Contents

List of Illustrations

Preface
to the Second Edition

Most people entering management for the first time, do so with little or no formal training. As a result, they rather tend to adopt the management styles by which they themselves were managed. Too often, this perpetuates poor or discredited management techniques.

This book has been written specifically for such people and for all those who intend to embark upon a management career in the near future.

Most managers, young and old, new and experienced, find that the hardest part of their job is the management of staff. With this in mind, this book is designed to help managers unravel the mysteries of dealing with people at work and to help them get the best from an invaluable resource and so become better managers.

This is a highly practical book, based largely upon the author's experiences as both a line manager and management trainer. It has been designed to be both easy to read and simple to refer back to.

Each chapter addresses a different topic, but they all have one thing in common — they involve people. Every area discussed is illustrated with examples and fictional mini case studies, to highlight the results of both good and bad practices. Checklists are used to emphasise the main points and to compare the right and wrong management techniques. Each chapter closes with questions and brief fictional case studies for discussion.

Having read this book, it is hoped that you will find ways of putting the good points into practice. Improvements will only happen if *you* make them happen.

Finally, I would like to thank all those many managers, both past and present, who have by their actions, contributed to the contents of this book.

John Humphries

IS THIS YOU?

Management trainee   Staff supervisor

Department Head

Business student   Production manager

Sales manager

Job applicant   Accountant

Works/factory manager

Retailer   Business owner

Transport manager

Head teacher   Hospital manager

Catering manager

Partner   Director

College principal

Hotelier   Office manager

Voluntary work organiser

Customer services manager   Training officer

Project manager

Instructor   Construction manager

Youth organiser

Police officer   Fire officer

Prison governor

Social worker   Military leader

Section head

Community group leader   Mentor

Banker   Resort manager   Lawyer

1
What is a Manager?

'So much of what we call management consists of making it difficult for people to work.' – Peter F Drucker.

'The secret of managing is to keep the guys who hate you away from the guys who are undecided.' – Casey Stengel.

'Management by objectives works if you know the objectives.' Ninety percent of the time you don't.' – Laurence J Peter.

THE BEGINNINGS OF MANAGEMENT

A form of management began when Man first employed others to work for him. In those early days, the relationship between employer and employee was that of master and servant, or landlord and serf. Workers were treated as chattels and motivation was based on the simple principle 'if you don't work, you don't eat'. Some people seem to believe that things have changed little since.

As the size of labour forces increased, bosses were obliged to employ others to manage their workers. Among the earliest examples of these 'employee managers' were the overseers engaged by the Pharoahs during the building of the pyramids in ancient Egypt.

Whilst slavery was legally abolished in Great Britain in 1833, it was not until the Trade Unions Act of 1872 that workers began to acquire rights and employers were forced to change their attitudes.

However, a few far-sighted men were already aware of the value of people in the workplace. In 1776, the economist Adam Smith wrote in his book *The Wealth of Nations* that wealth was derived principally from labour and that labour could be made more productive by specialisation. The Welsh reformer, Robert Owen (1771-1858) was instrumental in improving the conditions of workers and in 1813 opened his revolutionary new cotton mill in New Lanark. Later, a number of industrialists came to realise that people worked better if given the opportunity for a better lifestyle. To this end, in 1895 George Cadbury began the building of Bourneville, one of Britain's first 'green' suburbs.

Despite all of these changes, it was not until after World War Two that employers began really to appreciate how to manage their employees. Much of this was due to the work of American psychologists such as Maslow, MacGregor and Hetzberg. Although the theories put forward by these men are now seen to contain flaws, it is from them that modern management techniques have evolved.

We are still learning when it comes to managing people. Everyone is aware of the need to cut costs and increase profits. We are learning more and more clearly that these can best be achieved by good management of employees. Good management must start from the top, so remember, you are the senior managers of tomorrow.

ART OR SCIENCE?

The dictionary defines a **manager** as 'one who manages; person in charge of a business'. Turning to manage, we read 'have control of; be manager of; operate (a tool etc) effectively; deal with (a person) tactfully'. It is is this last definition that forms the theme of this book.

Is management an art or a science? In reality it is a combination of both, with a large helping of common sense. Management is a very specific function within business: it is not, as many people believe, something than can just be tacked on to day-to-day activities. It requires a completely different set of skills.

One of the common myths is that the manager should be the best exponent of the 'craft skills' within the department. In theory, a good manager should be able to manage any department within an organisation with the minimum of adaptation. Thus, instead of giving people titles such as sales manager or production manager, they might be better described as manager of sales or manager of production.

What makes a good manager? Many directors say that it is the person who can achieve objectives in the most cost effective manner. This may well satisfy the needs of the financial director and the shareholders, but those who practise this approach with little or no regard for other people can cause many problems for themselves and their company in the future. A good manager is one whose staff works *with* him rather than *for* him.

BECOMING A MANAGER

Can anyone become a manager? In theory yes, in practice no. Many people are unable or unwilling to adapt to the needs of management.

How do you become a manager? People are usually promoted for one of the following reasons:

- They are good at their present job.
- They have been with the company a long time.
- Their age gives them seniority.
- They know the right people.
- They happen to be in the right place at the right time.

Rarely are they promoted because they will make good managers.

As with most activities in life, you won't know how good you are until you really try it. If you want to go skiing, horse riding or mountaineering you can of course do so, but you would normally take a few lessons first. Management is no different so you should learn how to do it before taking such a major career step.

In some professions, for example the police, staff have to pass examinations before being considered for promotion into a management role. Whilst most of these exams are of a technical nature, some people-management skills are included. You, too, can take a management course, terminating with examinations and a qualification. These range from the Higher National Certificate in Business Studies to a Masters Degree in Business Administration. These are certainly very worthwhile endeavours, but the syllabuses concentrate on such areas as finance, marketing, or business strategy, with scant reference to the management of people. Thus, you may be highly qualified technically but if you are unable to manage your staff effectively, you will find it difficult to achieve the right results.

Responsibilities and duties of a manager

'To lead, motivate and develop the team to achieve the agreed objectives.' This kind of definition is often used in job descriptions to describe the responsibilities of a manager.

Every manager has responsibilities towards him or herself, their team, the individuals within the team, the company and the tasks in hand. Most managers find themselves under constant pressure to achieve targets as cost effectively as possible. In an effort to meet these demands, they too often forget the needs of the people for whom they are responsible. The results can be disastrous.

The duties of a manager are:

- To motivate staff to perform to the best of their abilities and to prevent demotivation.
- To delegate tasks, thus giving themselves more time to manage and develop staff.
- To plan and control the activities within their domain to ensure that objectives are met.
- To take decisions in order to help the team.
- To manage problems, not to solve them all, but to help the team reach acceptable solutions.
- To initiate and encourage ideas from the team.
- To develop the team. It is often said that a manager's first duty should be to develop a successor. If there is no-one capable of stepping into your shoes, you could be reducing your chances of further promotion.
- To recruit the right staff for the team.

Managing resources

Once you become a manager, the following resources will be at your disposal:

- People – acknowledged as being the most difficult resource to manage. They have different needs, attitudes, abilities and personalities. These are not constant and can change from day to day, hour to hour. A good manager will maximise the strengths and minimise the weaknesses.
- Time – the most democratic of the resources. Everyone has sixty seconds in a minute, sixty minutes in an hour etc. It is how this time is used that determines managerial effectiveness.
- Space – this is expensive and many work places suffer from a lack of it. However, much can be made of the space available to improve the working environment and people's behaviour.
- Finance – all managers will be involved with budgets and expenditure to some degree. Specialist books and training specifically designed to deal with finance for non-financial managers are available.
- Equipment – including desks, telephones, photocopiers and personal computers. You should ensure that your team have sufficient for their needs, while bearing in mind that idle equipment is a non-productive cost.
- Information – ensure that all information received is given the right priority and used as appropriate to help your team.

Their utilisation will affect your team and the individuals within the team, so managing these resources effectively is vital.

WHAT MAKES A GOOD MANAGER?

'Leaders are born and not made', says the famous quotation. Is it true? Indeed, is it true of managers who are, after all, leaders in their own right. Perhaps not entirely. Nevertheless, a manager should possess certain qualities that can be developed but not taught from scratch.

A survey was undertaken in 1987 in which staff in a large number of commercial and government organisations were asked to state the qualities that they sought in a manager. Although some fifty different qualities were identified, the following ten were constantly rated as being the most important:

Ten key qualities for managers

1. Providing clear directions by:
   - establishing clear goals and standards,
   - communicating group goals,
   - involving people in setting targets,
   - being clear and thorough when delegating tasks.
2. Encouraging open, two-way communication by:
   - being open and candid when dealing with people,
   - being honest, direct and to the point,
   - establishing a climate of openness and trust.
3. Willing to coach and support people by:
   - being supportive and helpful,
   - being constructive when correcting poor performance,
   - supporting the staff upwards.
4. Providing objective recognition by:
   - recognising good performance more often than criticising,
   - relating rewards to the excellence of performance.
5. Establishing on-going controls to
   - follow up on important issues and actions,
   - giving staff feedback on their performance.
6. Selecting the right people to staff the organisation.
7. Understanding the financial implications of decisions.
8. Encouraging innovation and new ideas.
9. Giving out clear cut decisions when necessary.
10. Constantly demonstrating high levels of integrity.

Are these the qualities you look for in your manager? If so, then your staff probably have similar aspirations. Management qualities can be divided into three groups:

- Attributes – in-born qualities; difficult to acquire unless there is something there to be developed.
- Skills – qualities that can be learned and developed.
- Knowledge – information learned and acquired.

Management qualitites

Below is a list of qualities that will help to make you an effective manager of people:

Attributes	Skills	Knowledge
Integrity	Communication	Staff needs
Flexibility	Listening	Company policy
Open mindedness	Motivation	Company procedures
Decisiveness	Delegation	Company objectives
Trustworthy	Innovation	Products/services
Unbiased	Training	Marketplace
Enthusiastic*	Planning	Competition
Imaginative	Controlling	Financial
Humorous	Influencing	

*Enthusiasm must be appropriate. Too much enthusiasm can be as dangerous as too little.

Don't worry if you do not possess everything in this list. If you did, you probably would not be reading this book. However, the more attributes you have, the easier it will be for you to manage people effectively.

Earning respect

To be effective as a manager, it is essential to have the respect of your staff, fellow managers and superiors. Respect does not come with the job title, it must be earned. It takes time to gain respect which is earned in the following stages:

Respect
Trust
Reliability
Open communication
Commitment to objectives

Unless you practise open communication and show a commitment to the company's objectives, you will have no chance of earning respect.

A reputation for reliability is earned by ensuring that you do those things that you say you will and by making decisions and sticking to them.

When people learn that you will not divulge confidences, you will gain their trust.

Respect will be the result of continuous practice of the other four.

MANAGEMENT THEORIES

As previously mentioned, modern management techniques were first developed in the 1950s. Since then, there have been a welter of management theories, many of them propounded by academics and psychologists. One which came into vogue in the early 1960s was **Management by Objectives** (MBO). In simple terms, managers were expected to set themselves a series of objectives and their effectiveness was measured by their ability to reach these objectives within a pre-determined time scale. Unfortunately their objectives rarely took account of the people for whom they were responsible.

In the early 1970s, the purchasing manager of a manufacturing company, decided to practise MBO to reduce wastage and thus save his company money. Unfortunately, he became so obsessed with this goal, that within a few months, the stockholding of components had been so drastically reduced, that the company were unable to complete several large orders on time. As a result they lost valuable business and the purchasing manager lost his job!

As with many of these 'flavour of the month' theories, it has tended to fall by the wayside due largely to the reason quoted by Laurence J Peter at the beginning of this chapter.

The references to objectives in the sections on Qualities of a Manager and Respect, means being aware of the overall company objective. This could be to increase the market share by x percent within y time scale; to maintain profit as a percentage of sales at its present level, and so on.

Contrary to the quotation from the management guru, Peter F Drucker, management should consist of making it easier for people to work. Hopefully, Casey Stengel's quote was made with tongue in cheek. By employing good management techniques, there should be very few colleagues who hate you, only the envious ones.

CASE STUDIES — AN INTRODUCTION

Let us now introduce three managers whose careers we will be
following in the succeeding chapters. Each employs a different style of
management; we will observe the effects on their staff of their
techniques in a variety of situations.

Arthur Rowe, Sales Manager

Arthur Rowe is the Sales Manager with an engineering company
based in the Midlands. Arthur is in his mid-fifties and has been with
the company for twenty-two years, the last fifteen in his present post.
He has never received any formal management training and considers
himself to be a manager of the 'old school'. At present he controls a
team of six salesmen, a sales clerk and a secretary. Over the years, he
has been very successful in winning business for his company and
keeps most of the major accounts for himself. He employs a 'watch
my lips' style of management and if he has a philosophy it is that
there is a job to be done and if the staff don't like it, tough. Staff
turnover in his department is high.

David Wilson, Social Services Manager

Three years ago David Wilson was promoted to manager of the social
services department of a local authority in the West Country. He is
thirty years old, married with four children. After leaving university
with a degree in history, he worked for a large charity and another
local authority before securing his present position. He likes to
describe himself as a 'people person' and his main aim at work is to
ensure that his staff of ten are happy. He often takes on extra
casework so as not to overload them. David has regular staff meetings
and likes to involve his team in every aspect relating to the
department. Although he is well liked by his team, they do consider
him weak when it comes to making decisions. When he gets the time,
he is determined to attend a management course.

Liz Cole, Front of House Manager

Liz Cole is the Front of House Manager with a major hotel chain.
Now in her late twenties, Liz has been in the hotel industry since
leaving catering college. She has worked her way up the promotion
ladder, attending various management courses on the way. For the
last two years she has worked at a large hotel in London, where she is
in charge of reception, reservations and porterage. Liz has two
'assistant managers', a head receptionist and a head porter reporting

to her. Although she is younger than many of her team, she is well respected and considered by them to be firm but fair.

SUMMARY

Good management practices
- Open, two-way communication.
- Be aware that everyone is different.
- Earn respect.
- Balance the needs of your staff and the tasks to be completed.
- Manage all resources judiciously.
- Allocate sufficient time to manage within the normal working week.

Bad management practices
- Closed door policy.
- Treat staff as homogeneous group.
- Demand respect.
- Achieving the objective is everything.
- Ensure the staff are content, regardless.
- Expand the working week to accommodate both 'doing' and 'managing'.

DISCUSSION POINTS

1. What difficulties are you likely to face if you are promoted to manage your former peers? How could you overcome these problems?

2. You have secured a position of sales administration manager with a company for whom you have not worked before. Upon meeting your team for the first time, you are greeted with some hostility. You discover that they have not had a manager for the last three months. Bill Atkinson, who is older than you and has been with the company for many years, expected to be promoted. He has acted as 'unofficial manager' during the interim. The rest of your staff still look to him for help and advice. What steps can you take to establish your position as manager?

3. How would you interpret 'commitment to objectives' in your present job?

2
How to Manage Yourself

SPOKEN FROM EXPERIENCE

'Healthy self-criticism and an abiding willingness to learn seems to me to be the most important requirements of any manager' — HRH Prince Philip.

'The difference between a job and a career is the difference between 40 and 60 hours a week' — Robert Frost.

QUALITY NOT QUANTITY

Before trying to manage others, it is vital to know how to manage yourself. If you are seen to be disorganised, easily pressured, blinkered in your views, unmotivated and subject to swift changes of mood, you will not win the respect and credibility of your staff.

Do you agree with the above quotation from the American poet Robert Frost? If so, then you must ask yourself what you will do with the additional twenty hours. Self management is not about the amount of time you spend on an activity, but about what you do during that time. It's quality that counts, not quantity.

Time is very easily wasted but impossible to regain. Time spent on non-management activity is not necessarily unproductive time. But could the time have been better used elsewhere?

MANAGING OR DOING

One of the most difficult aspects of making the transition into management is knowing how to allocate your time between 'managing' and 'doing', ie continuing to practice your technical or craft skills.

The following diagrams illustrate the difference between the 'amateur' manager and the 'professional'.

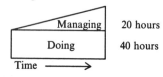

The 'amateur' will continue to do pre-management tasks and, realising that he also has to manage, expand his working week to cope.

The 'professional' will spend less time doing and more time managing as experience grows.

How much of your time do you spend managing and how much doing? The longer the hours you work in order to do both, the more likely you are to become stressed. This will have a detrimental effect on you, your family and your staff.

What is the difference between managing and doing?

Below is a list of activities. Tick only those you think are managing:

(a) Visiting one of your company's customers to sort out a problem. _____

(b) Deciding whether to add to the staff total. _____

(c) Approving a request from one of your staff for a routine expenditure. _____

(d) Reviewing monthly reports to determine progress towards achieving specific objectives for your area of responsibility. _____

(e) Gathering the information required to prepare a report on your department's expenditure. _____

(f) Deciding what the cost budget will be for your area of responsibility. _____

(g) Attending an industry conference to learn the latest in technical developments. _____

(h) Meeting with an outside specialist to design a profit sharing scheme. _____

(i) Explaining to one of your staff why he/she is not receiving a salary increase. _____

(j) Giving a talk to the local chamber of commerce about your company's plans and purpose. _____

(k) Asking one of your staff what they think about an idea you have for their area of responsibility. _____

(l) Entertaining the manager of a large company with
     whom you are negotiating.   _____

Only (b), (d), (f), (i) and (k) are true management tasks. The
remainder could just as easily be done by other members of your staff.
   If you have ticked 9 or more, then you have a good understanding
of the manager's role; 8 or less, then read on.

IMPROVING YOURSELF

As suggested in the quotation by HRH Prince Philip, managers
should be willing to learn. Part of self management is accepting that
you do not know everything and being prepared to learn and adapt.
   There are four stages in the learning process:

1. Unconscious incompetence.
2. Conscious incompetence.
3. Conscious competence.
4. Unconscious competence.

   Let's illustrate this with the analogy of learning to drive a car.

1. Before starting to learn, you probably thought that it would be
    very easy. After all, it looks simple.
2. Once you began to take lessons, you soon realised that there was
    more to it. You thought that you would never master the skills of
    having to cope with the clutch, gears, steering and the mirror all at
    the same time.
3. Having passed your driving test, you were probably acutely
    conscious of every action that you took for the next few months.
4. As time passed and you became more experienced, these actions
    became automatic and now you drive without really thinking
    about it.

   The same can be said for management. It may have looked easy
from the outside. You are probably now at the second stage. By
reading and practising the techniques described in this book, you will
soon progress to stage three. As you gain more experience, it will
become second nature.

Analyse yourself
An important part of self management, is the ability to analyse your

strengths and weaknesses. Write down a list of those things in which you are competent and a second list of those areas that need improvement. Be honest, don't kid yourself.

Concentrate on improving the weaker areas. Don't be afraid to ask for help from others ensuring beforehand that they are competent. Read books on management skills and adapt them for your own use as appropriate.

MANAGING PRESSURE

Never allow yourself to be put under unreasonable pressure. Too often those above will pass more and more work down to you. The more you accept the more you will get, until you find yourself under unacceptable pressure. As a result you will exert more pressure on your staff. Your organisation and planning will go by the board and you will be running faster and faster just to remain in the same place.

Be aware of any such impending pressures and learn to say 'no'. Providing that you have plans and priorities that fill the working week when your boss attempts to pass on extra tasks be prepared to tell him that you are unable to accept them. If he insists, ask him to prioritise your revised workload. You must be firm, you owe it to your staff as well as yourself. The first sign of weakness on your part and you are doomed for the future.

'GAMES PLAYING'

Beware of becoming involved in playing 'games'. There are three specific 'games' that many managers play.

'Look at me'
This is designed to draw attention to the person playing it.

The personnel manager of an engineering company had an office on the same floor as the directors strategically placed opposite the lift. He ensured that he arrived early each morning, invariably ate lunch at his desk and was among the last to leave in the evening. His office door was left open all day so that everyone who passed by could see how conscientious he was. One day the managing director asked him why he spent so much time in the office. The personnel manager was lost for a plausible reply. His ploy had been uncovered.

'The harrassed executive'
From the day he was appointed, a junior manager in the administration department of a computer company, travelled to

and from work every day with a bulging briefcase. Sometimes he took two such cases home at weekends. The fact that they were never opened at home did not come into the equation. He hoped to give the impression of being a dedicated, overworked, harrassed executive. Very few people were taken in.

'Meetings mania'

The director of an oil company was an expert at this game. He ensured that he received an invitation to every meeting in which he might have an interest, however tenuous. He arranged meetings with his staff on a daily basis. If there was no specific purpose, he would refer to it as a 'review meeting'. When he was not actually in a meeting, he could be seen scurrying along the corridors clutching armfuls of paper and files. Not surprisingly, when the company had to make redundancies, he was among the first to go.

These games are all designed to impress other people. Don't be tempted to join in.

MANAGING YOUR EMOTIONS

It is very important to learn to control your emotions at work. Highly emotional people are often labelled as unstable, untrustworthy and weak. None of these are traits associated with good management.

Learn not to show any negative emotions resulting from events at work. You may not agreed with certain actions or decisions taken by your superiors. If that is the case discuss it rationally with them, never moan or complain to your staff. If you are seen to be demotivated, it will have a contagious effect on those you manage.

Similarly, control your temper. It may only take you moments to lose it but could take days, even weeks, to regain the respect of your staff.

If you ever feel it necessary to reprimand one of your employees, never do it in public. It will certainly damage your reputation if you do.

Beware of false or over enthusiasm. This does not mean that you have to remain completely neutral. There is nothing wrong with expressing positive feelings, providing they are genuine.

Traits well worth cultivating include an even temperament, equanimity, fair mindedness and self discipline. Remember, a smile can be infectious.

DISCUSSION POINTS

1. List your strengths and weaknesses. How are you going to improve the latter?

2. Identify those things that cause you undue pressure. How can you help to reduce this pressure?

3. After you have read this book and the case studies, write down the strengths and weaknesses of Arthur Rowe, David Wilson and Liz Cole.

'According to the training manager
I'm still at the unconscious incompetence stage.'

3
How to Communicate with People

SPOKEN FROM EXPERIENCE

'The two words 'information' and 'communication' are often used interchangeably, but they signify quite different things. Information is giving out; communication is getting through' – Sidney J Harris.

'For years employee communications meant bowling scores, personal items, and similar information not related to the company's business. Then somebody had the good sense to ask the employees what they really wanted, and they overwhelmingly said that they wanted to be informed on developments of all types around the company' – Don G Mitchell.

'Precision of communication is important, more important than ever, in our era of hair-trigger balances, when a false or misunderstood word may create as much disaster as a sudden thoughtless act' – James Thurber.

TRANSMITTING YOUR MESSAGE

Good verbal communication is a two-way process: the speaker gives the listeners the opportunity to ask questions and make comments about what has been said in order to clarify or query the statement. Failure to do so, means that the communication becomes merely information giving, as suggested above by Sidney J Harris.

The objective of verbal communication is to transmit a message so that it is understood by the listener. This involves a specific process as illustrated in Figure 1.

The speaker has to put his message into words (**encode**). These words are then uttered through filters or barriers, and the result is then decoded by the listener. The better the encoding and the fewer the filters, the greater the likelihood that the listener will receive the correct message.

If the listener makes no comments, when appropriate the speaker should invite the person to do so. Never say 'Do you understand?' as this puts the onus on the listener and rather than appear foolish, they will say 'Yes'. If you say 'Have I made myself clear?' then the responsibility rests with you and, the listener is more likely to ask for further clarification. It is only a matter of words.

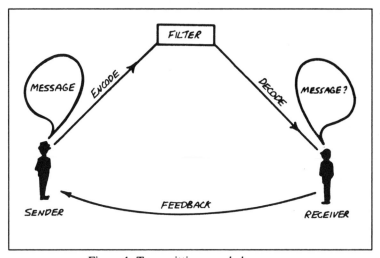

Figure 1. Transmitting a verbal message.

COMMUNICATION FILTERS

When we filter coffee the grounds are left behind on the filter paper and only the liquid goes into the jug. A similar thing happens with communication. There are three types of filters which only allow a proportion of the message to get through. As a result, we only receive part of the message, and often, only the part that we want to hear.

Attention filters
Physical distractions such as:

- Noise – other people talking, telephones ringing, traffic, music.
- Environmental – too hot, too cold, poor lighting.
- Interruptions – people, telephones.
- Timing – trying to talk to someone when they are about to go somewhere or are in the middle of a job.

Emotional filters
These are inherent in the speaker or listener and probably unknown to the other person.

- Prejudice – dislike of the other person, the way they are dressed, the message itself.

- Status – the other person is higher or lower in the company hierachy which can affect the way in which you speak and listen to them.

- Experience – if previous communication with a person has resulted in an unpleasant experience, you will be wary when approaching them the next time, not wishing to repeat the experience.

- Assumptions – assuming what the message will be and thus not listening properly.

- Values and beliefs – we all have our own codes regarding morals, religion, politics and so on. If the message transgresses these standards, we are likely to switch off.

Word filters
Certain words and phrases can cause us to stop listening to the person who utters them.

- Criticism – few of us like to be criticised. 'That was the wrong way to tackle the problem.'

- Moralising – 'You shouldn't have done that.'

- Ordering – 'I want the report on my desk by Thursday afternoon without fail.'

- Threatening – 'If you don't do what I say, you will be in serious trouble.'

- Advising – 'I suggest that you...'. People will only accept the advice that agrees with their solution. They will respond to advice with the phrase 'Yes, but'.

- Logical argument – it is too difficult to argue with logic.

- Reassuring – 'Never mind, everything will turn out all right in the end.'

- Diverting – 'Yes all right, but as I was saying...'.

- Jargon – unless the listener understands the jargon, they will wonder what it means and will not be listening to the rest of the message.

What other filters can you add to the those given above?

Reducing the filters

Even one filter can reduce the effect or distort communication but in most instances, two or more are operating at the same time. Being aware that they exist, is half the battle in reducing the effect of filters.

It is not always possible or practical to eliminate attention filters, but they *can* be reduced. If the proposed conversation will take more than a few minutes, find somewhere quiet to hold it and let it be known that you want no interruptions. It is simple enough to get your timing right. If someone approaches you at an inconvenient time, politely tell them so and arrange to meet later.

You can do little about other peoples' emotions, but try to put your own on hold when talking and listening to others. If you sense emotional filters becoming barriers, keep your conversation brief and to the point.

Take care over the words and phrases that you use. How would you respond as the listener? If you are on the receiving end, question the speaker, ask him to justify his comments.

HOW TO SPEAK EFFECTIVELY

Verbal communication can be broken down into three distinct elements:

- word,
- tone of voice,
- non-verbal or body language.

Research has shown that each has a specific value in transmitting the 'true' message:

- words 7%
- tone 35%
- non-verbal 58%

You may disagree with these percentages, but think about it for a moment.

You have complete control over the words that you use. You have less control over the tone as your emotion begins to take over. Try saying the phrase 'Where did you go last night?' without emphasising any of the words. Repeat it, putting an emphasis on the first word, then again, this time emphasising the word 'you'. Three different 'true' messages will be conveyed to the listener and they will respond accordingly. You have virtually no control over the non-verbal, your body language. Subconsciously your body will reveal what you really mean and think.

If you sit with your arms and legs crossed, this is defensive posture and indicates a hostile attitude towards the other person and/or the message. Sitting with your arms folded with your thumbs up, shows a superior attitude. Leaning forward indicates either interest or intimidation. People who rest their chin on one hand and have a finger in or near their mouth, need reassurance. Those who rub their chins are thinking or making a decision and will not be listening to you, so stop talking. Read Allan Pease's book *Body Language* for more examples.

Gestures are intentional movements and should not be confused with body language.

You may be able to control your body language at the beginning of a conversation, but the more you become involved, the more your subconscious will take over.

To back up the importance of body language in verbal communication, it should be noted that of information relayed to the brain 87% is via the eyes, 9% is via the ears, and 4% is via the other senses (taste, touch etc).

Helpful hints
The main points to remember to help you in your verbal communication are:

- Tone – use the right tone; try to suppress inappropriate emotions.

- Words – avoid word filters; don't use long words simply to impress.

- Non-verbal – be aware of the other person's body language and attempt to overcome negative postures by changing your words, tone and posture.

- Clarify – ensure that you speak clearly and don't mumble or shout.

- Speed – speak at an even pace, neither too quickly nor too slowly.

- Emphasise – don't speak in a monotone. Emphasise the important points and eliminate affectations such as dropping your voice at the end of sentences.

- Jargon – if you feel the necessity to use jargon, make sure that your listener is familiar with the terms you use.

ASKING QUESTIONS

As Carl T Rowan said, 'There aren't any embarrassing questions – just embarrassing answers'. Questions form a large part of any conversation. The way in which the question is asked will colour the response received.

You have probably been told in the past that questions are either 'closed' and will only be answered with a yes or no, or 'open' beginning with how, why, what, when and so on and must invite a longer answer. However, it is the tone in which the question is asked which will largely determine the type of response. A closed question asked in a calm manner will usually elicit an explanatory answer. Conversely, an open question asked in an aggressive tone will probably get an equally aggressive reply.

Question categories

There are categories of questions which can be used depending upon the type of information that you want in return.

- Elaboration questions – for information of a general nature, for example:
  'Tell me about...'
  'Is there anything more?'
  'Would you elaborate on that please?'

- Specification questions – asking for more detailed information.
  'What precisely did she say?'
  'When was the last time this happened?'

- Feelings questions – asked when you want to know the emotional effect of something.
  'What did you feel when it happened?'
  'How do you feel when people are aggressive toward you?'

- Opinion questions – most people hold opinions about things and welcome the opportunity to express them.
  'What do you like about your present job?'
  'What do you least like about your job?'
  'What would you like that you don't have?'

- Behavioural questions – past behaviour is a good indicator of future behaviour.

    'How would you usually deal with a situation like this?'
    'What did you do the last time this happened?'
    'How did you react when...?'

Warnings

Bear the following points in mind when asking questions of members of your staff:

- Too many questions from you will appear to be an interrogation of the other person.

- When you ask a question, keep quiet and wait for the answer. Don't be tempted to re-phrase your question unless asked to.

- Ask one question at a time. If you ask multiple questions you will only get one or two answers.

- If you don't get a full answer to a question, ask it again.

- Listen carefully to the answers.

- Refrain from asking leading questions: 'You would agree wouldn't you that...?', except when seeking agreement.

LISTENING

'The art of effective listening is essential to clear communication, and clear communication is necessary to management successs. Since the biggest part of your job as an executive consists of getting things done through people, it will pay you to learn how to become a good listener if you aren't one already' – J C Penny.

When you were young, you were taught to speak, to read and to write. How many of you had lessons in how to listen? Although it is such a vital part of good communiction, people pay little attention to improving their listening skills.

Hearing is not the same as listening. We hear all sorts of noises during every waking moment but we do not listen to them. Hearing is reactive, listening requires a positive effort. A sure sign of when a person has not been listening to you, is when they reply 'I hear what you are saying'.

It is not enough to listen by concentrating, although this is important, you need to relay to the speaker that you have been listening.

REFLECTIVE SKILLS

The simplest way of indicating that you have listened to the speaker is by employing reflective techniques. Reflection is a form of summary of what has been said. It demonstrates empathy with the speaker.

Our responses fall into one of three types:

- Apathy – dismissive, showing a lack of interest in what has been said.
- Sympathy – sharing the feeling of others; allowing their problem to become your problem.
- Empathy – showing that you appreciate the other person's feelings or point of view without becoming involved or agreeing with them.

Example

A friend says to you 'I am a bit down at the moment. My cat died yesterday. He was a lovely old chap and a real companion. I am going to miss him.'

Apathetic response: 'Really, anyway as I was saying...' or 'Why don't you get another one?'.

Sympathetic response: 'I know how you must feel, I felt dreadful for weeks after our dog passed away last year'.

Empathetic response: 'You must feel very upset'.

Reflecting facts is a matter of summarising the information and feeding it back to the speaker. For instance, 'Although I've written letters and made numerous telephone calls to Briggs & Co. they still haven't paid the £2,000 that they owe us. So I'm going to London tomorrow to see them face to face and sort it out once and for all.' 'You believe that personal contact will be more effective.' Nothing is added to the content when reflecting facts.

Reflecting feelings is more difficult as you must capture the right emotion. 'I really thought that I'd get promotion when John left. I should have done, I've been here for five years and have got the right experience. In fact I used to take over from him when he went on holiday. I'm fed up.'

'You must feel sad' – wrong response.

'You must feel disappointed' – right response.

There are times when you can reflect both facts and feelings.

'You know I've written to the council, phoned my local councillor and even written to the papers but all to no avail. The streets are still filthy with paper, cartons from fast food shops and dog muck. It's a disgrace. What on earth must visitors to the town think of us?'

'You feel frustrated because the authorities appear to be doing nothing to improve the situation.'

You feel...[emotion]...because/since/when...[facts]...

When you reflect facts and/or feelings, stay silent and allow the other person to speak. They may well give you more information. This technique is particularly effective when dealing with complaints as it allows the complainant to let off steam without your attempting to argue or defend yourself. When the outburst is finished, you can ask relevant questions to establish the facts.

Example

'You said that you would deliver our order on Tuesday; it's now Thursday and I'm still waiting. We have had to completely reorganise our production schedules and contact our customers to explain why we can't deliver to them on time.'

Wrong response

(a) 'You feel annoyed because we haven't delivered your goods on time.'

   'Annoyed, I'm absolutely livid...'

(b) 'We promised delivery on Tuesday but you haven't received your order yet.'

   'That's just what I've said, isn't it'?

Right response

'The late delivery has caused you a difficulty with your production' – ignore the emotion in this instance.

   'Yes it has. What are you going to do?'

At this point you can ask questions to gather all the facts surrounding the matter.

In order to reflect correctly, you must listen carefully to what is being said. It is a technique that takes practice but will help to improve your listening skills.

CASE STUDIES

What will be the likely effect on those involved in the following conversations?

Impatient Arthur

Arthur Rowe called one of his salesmen into his office. 'Right Thompson, I'm not satisfied with your efforts. Only one order in the last two weeks and you've only made five appointments. It's not good enough. What are you going to do about it?'

'Well, I've tried but people aren't really interested.'

'I don't want any lame excuses. I want you to make at least three appointments before the end of the day. All right?'

'Yes, but...'

'No buts, just get on with it and see me before you go home.'

David is laid back

One of David Wilson's team has come to him with a work related problem.

'I've been trying to get Mrs Green into a council nursing home but they say that because she has a few savings, she is going to have to pay and she really can't afford it.'

'I know, it's difficult, isn't it? I had a similar case last year.'

'So what can we do?'

'Why don't you suggest that Mrs Green gives her savings to her children?'

'Yes, but she's only got one son and he doesn't take much interest in his mother.'

'Really, anyway leave it a while, I'm sure it will sort itself out.'

Liz talks it through

Liz Cole was approached by one of her reservation staff. 'I've got a problem. About two months ago, I had a phone call from a company booking twenty-five rooms for a sales conference. They didn't send anything in writing and they have just phoned again to check that everything is OK. The conference is next week and we don't have enough rooms for them.'

'They didn't send any written confirmation?'

'No.'

'You told them that it was necessary when you spoke to them the first time?'

'Oh, yes. I always do with every telephone booking.'

'Good. What can we do to help them?'

'Well, we've got fifteen rooms and we could try and get them accommodation for the rest at one of the nearby hotels.'

'That's a good idea.'

'Right, I'll phone them back and put it to them.'

DISCUSSION POINTS

1. List any prejudices you hold against people with whom you have to communicate at work. What can you do to overcome them?

2. Write your reflections to the following statements:
(a) 'I'm supposed to be going on holiday next week, but unless I can find someone to look after the dogs, I'll have to cancel it.'
(b) 'I'm fed up with the way you are always putting me down in front of the others.'
(c) 'The traffic gets worse every day. I have to leave earlier and earlier to get into work on time.'

How to Conduct Staff Appraisals
A Practical Handbook for Every Manager

Nigel Hunt

Managers and organisations neglect staff appraisal at their peril today. But what exactly is staff appraisal? Is it something to be welcomed or feared? Why is it now so vital, and what are the benefits? Should senior as well as junior staff undergo appraisal, and how could this be done? Which managers should do the appraisals, and how should they start? This book, now in a new edition, sets out a basic framework which every manager can use or adapt, whether in business and industry, transport, education, health and public services. 'Informative... Points for discussion and case studies are prominent throughout... the case studies are highly relevant and good.' *Progress (NEBS Management Association Journal)*.

£8.99, 154pp illus. 1 85703 117 2. 2nd edition.

Please add postage & packing (UK £1 per copy, Europe £2 per copy, World £3 per copy airmail).

How To Books Ltd, Plymbridge House, Estover Road, Plymouth, PL6 7PZ,United Kingdom.
Tel: (01752) 697545. Fax: (01752) 695699. Telex: 45635.

4
How to Motivate People

SPOKEN FROM EXPERIENCE

'The secret principle of human nature is the craving to be appreciated' – William James.

'Everybody wants to be considered somebody. Make them feel important' – Anon.

'Treat 'em like dogs, and you'll have dogs' work and dogs' actions. Treat 'em like men and you'll have mens' work' – Harriet Beecher Stowe.

WHY PEOPLE ARE MOTIVATED

More has been written and more theories propounded on the subject of motivation than any other area of the management of people. However, much of this material is too theoretical to be of use to the average manager. This chapter is devoted to the practical ways in which you can motivate your staff.

The behaviour and actions of people are prompted by needs which require satisfying. In order to provide this satisfaction, it is necessary to identify the needs.

Nobody does anything unless they have a need. Simple everyday actions such as getting up, eating breakfast and cleaning your teeth are prompted by needs. Performing these actions, satisfies those needs.

If our needs remain unfulfilled, we establish a goal, consciously or subconsciously, and take the right actions to achieve that goal. We may wish to buy a car or take a holiday, so we do everything to satisfy these needs. However, as we shall see later, these are only superficial needs. Real needs are more deeply rooted.

The human being is a very complex animal and its needs are different for each individual. A further complication is that peoples' needs change on an irregular basis, either because they have been satisfied or more important ones have taken their place.

We observe behaviour in others, draw conclusions and make assumptions about their needs. The mistake made by many managers is trying to motivate by means of satisfying these assumed needs.

HOW PEOPLE ARE MOTIVATED

A common myth is that everybody is motivated by money. When disagreeing with this statement, most people say 'but everyone wants money!' There lies the difference. Needs are essential; wants are desirable. It is true that everyone needs a certain amount of money, enough to keep them in the style to which they have become accustomed. They may need more if there is something specific that they wish to buy, but not everyone falls into that category. So, people will only need money when their need for it has not been satisfied.

As a manager, you have certain tasks and actions that you require your staff to undertake. In order to be able to motivate them to do so, you must know and understand the needs of each member of your team. Because of the parameters in which you operate, you may be unable to satisfy the surface needs such as more money or promotion. Therefore you have to look for the subconscious needs that these represent and try to satisfy the person concerned by other means.

To one degree or another, everyone has the following subconscious needs.

The need for recognition
This is the most important motivational factor. We all need to be recognised by others for what we are. Almost everything we do is done to satisfy the need for recognition. When we are promoted, our worth is being recognised by our company. Buying a large house or car is an attempt to see the recognition from others that we have 'made it'. We join clubs, societies and do voluntary work so that we are recognised as being a valuable member of society. However, many of us neither recognise nor accept that this is our real need. Both the anonymous quotation and the one from Williams James, bear out this need.

The need for respect
It is our birthright to be accepted and respected as an individual person. As a manager you can satisfy this need by simply listening to your staff and expressing an interest in them as individuals. Too many managers still operate as indicated in the first part of the quotation by Harriet Beecher Stowe.

The need for responsibility

Most people yearn for responsibility, by having a task, however small, for which they are totally responsible and accountable. This is best achieved by delegation.

The need for reward

Not necessarily in the form of money, prizes or time off. So often this can be satisfied by a simple but genuine word of praise.

Respect, responsibility and reward are only means of gaining recognition.

The only needs we have that do not involve recognition are those that the American psychologist Abraham Maslow called **phsyiological needs**, such as eating, drinking and sleeping.

The simplest way of discovering the needs of each member of your team, is with regular, two-way communication.

PRACTICAL MOTIVATION AT WORK

Having said that you should get to know the needs of each of your staff, it is safe to say that they will all have a need for recognition. However, the way in which this can be satisfied may differ in each case. Here is a list of practical activities that you can do to help satisfy the need for recognition:

- Open, two-way communication.
- Good delegation (poor delegation can be demotivating).
- Involvement in decisions.
- Giving support and help.
- Recognising the need for privacy.
- Encouraging ideas and suggestions.
- Reducing stress.
- Exchanging information.
- Developing the staff.
- Enabling people to use their capabilities.
- Treating people as adults; with respect; as intelligent; as important.
- Giving sincere praise for a job well done.
- Praising effort. Don't always wait until a task has been completed before giving praise. Similarly, even if the result is not perfect, praise what is right. This will encourage that person to do even better in the future.

Sticks and carrots

'A few may nibble at the carrot, but all will duck to avoid the stick' –
Anon. This refers to the outdated view of motivation which, alas, is
still employed in many organisations. the carrot represents the
incentives offered to encourage people to work better; the stick is the
threat of what will happen to those who do not perform to standard.
Both methods can have disastrous results for all concerned.

Incentives

We all know managers whose philosophy is 'give them an incentive,
that will get them going'. However, this is no longer true, if it ever
was.

The dangers of incentives, whether they be cash, a crate of wine or a
Caribbean holiday, are:

- People will decide whether or not they need the prize. If they
  already have a video recorder, they are unlikely to be motivated
  by the prospect of winning another one.

- People will compare the value of the incentive with the extra
  effort required to win it and decide whether or not to compete.

- Once people discover that they are too far behind the leaders in
  the race, they will give up and become demotivated.

- There will only be one motivated winner and many demotivated
  losers.

- Incentive schemes are measured on results and do not take
  account of effort.

- As it is normally the sales departments that are offered such
  prizes, it can have a demotivating effect on the rest of the
  company.

When people do decide to try to win an incentive prize, it will be for
one of two reasons:

- To win the actual prize – reward.
- To be seen by others as the winner – recognition.

Example

A large home improvements company decided to implement a 'new' incentive scheme to motivate its team of forty commission only sales people. There were to be twenty-five prizes, ranging from a new car down to a £10 gift voucher. At the end of the incentive period, the top sales person would receive twenty-five tickets, the next, twenty-four and so on down to the twenty-fifth who would get just one ticket. At the annual dinner, these tickets would be put into a drum, the first one drawn out would win the first prize, the second ticket, the second prize and so on. The idea behind the scheme was to try and overcome the third and fourth dangers listed above.

When the time for the draw arrived, a new rule was introduced. Each sales person could only win one prize. The twelfth-placed sales person won the car and the twenty-third won a dish washer. The top salesperson won six bottles of claret. In fact the top five sales people only won minor prizes and they were extremely demotivated. As a result, the six sales people who had topped the list left the company and joined its competitors. So, whatever you do, you can't win!

Making incentives work
One way of handling incentives, is to award them after the event with no pre-announcement. Thus when someone puts forward an idea which is acted upon, they can be given a gift as a form of material recognition. Similarly, you could set intermediate targets which are known only to you. As each member of your team reaches these targets, you can reward them with a small gift. Teamwork can be encouraged by giving prizes of equal value to each team member when specific goals have been achieved.

Fear as a motivator
Commonly known as the 'big stick' method, this simply means threatening people with dire consequences, such as the sack, if they fail to achieve targets or standards. The danger of employing such a method is that you do not know how the person under threat will react until it is too late. They may respond by working harder to avoid the consequences, or they may decide to use the time available to seek another job. You can be sure that if they chose the first option, they will only work sufficiently well to reach the target and no more.

Any manager who uses the big stick will quickly lose any respect already gained. It is the sign of a weak and desperate manager.

Non-motivators
Many companies and organisations try to motivate their staff by improving the working conditions. Laudable though such actions are,

all that they do is satisfy expectations and wants. They fail to account for individual needs.

Non-motivators include:

- Salary increases – these are expected by the staff.
- Company cars – regarded by some as a perk, by others as a 'tool of the trade'.
- Improvements in the environment; more space, modern equipment, better restaurant facilities etc. The effect will be to stop people complaining until they want even more.

Occasionally these non-motivators can backfire on the company.

Example
A large financial institution decided to implement an awards for excellence scheme in an attempt to motivate its staff. It was to be held on an annual basis. Awards would be made in a wide variety of categories including best sales person; best computer operator; best cost-saving ideas and best support department. Nominations would be made in each category and an independent panel of judges would determine the winners. The award ceremony was to take place with an elaborate dinner at a top London hotel, hosted by a well known 'personality'. These awards were greeted with great enthusiasm in the first year. However, as with any incentive scheme, these were a few motivated winners and a host of demotivated losers. As a result the scheme lost its credibility and was treated with derision by most of the staff. By the third year, people were even refusing to be nominated and this costly exercise had to be abandoned. Oscars may have their place in the entertainment industry but are rarely appropriate in the commercial world.

This is not to say that companies should *not* improve working conditions, but they should not expect an increase in productivity and profits as a result.

DEMOTIVATION AND HOW TO AVOID IT

As a manager you should keep your eyes open for any signs of demotivation among your staff: it can be very contagious. Demotivation is usually manifested by a change in behaviour and signs to look out for include:

- absenteeism
- lateness

- shoddy work
- non-communication
- non-participation
- sudden outbursts of anger

Anyone who engages in any of the above does so for a reason, to gain attention. As a general rule people would rather be reprimanded than ignored. Thus anybody who suddenly starts taking time off, or becomes uncommunicative, will continue with this behaviour until their manager brings it to their attention. If as their manager you ignore these signs, you do so at your peril. The person concerned will become more and more demotivated and may eventually take more drastic action such as spreading malicious rumours, being disruptive or handing in their notice. None of these will reflect well on you.

The reasons why people become demotivated include:

- Lack of recognition – the most frequent cause.
- Boredom – work is unsufficiently interesting to stimulate them.
- Lack of involvement in decisions, changes and so on.
- Ideas neither encouraged nor listened to.
- Lack of development – no delegation or training.
- Constant criticism of performance with no praise for effort.
- Too much work – unable to cope, feels under pressure.

How can you help to prevent demotivation among your staff? —by development and practising good people management skills such as:

- good communication.
- delegating and training.
- involving the staff in decisions.
- encouraging ideas and suggestions.
- giving sincere praise when due.
- treating people as individuals.
- criticising constructively.

Example
Mary was a clerk in a Customs & Excise office. She was considered to be a hard and conscientious worker. After three years she experienced a serious domestic problem, and was unable to concentrate fully on her work. As a result, errors crept in for which she was reprimanded by her supervisor. Soon afterwards she developed migraines and took more and more sick leave. As her work continued to deteriorate she

became more demotivated and received more criticism from her superiors. She was threatened with dismissal if things did not improve. Mary became increasingly stressed and eventually suffered a nervous breakdown, spending several months in hospital and losing her job in the process.

If only her supervisors had recognised the changes in her behaviour and acted quickly, the problem could have been resolved and Mary would still be a valuable employee.

When a manager is doing everything possible to prevent demotivation among his staff and a member of his team shows any of the signals mentioned above, the cause is probably outside the work place. In such cases, the manager should arrange a **counselling interview** to try and discover the cause and reach an acceptable solution. (See Chapter 10 on Interviewing.)

CASE STUDIES

Arthur's own worst enemy – himself
The walls of Arthur Rowe's office are decorated with large graphs, one per salesman. On these are marked, in coloured inks, the total number of telephone calls, appointments and orders made by each salesman, each week. The graphs are clearly visible to everyone who enters his office, staff and customers alike.

At nine o'clock every morning, he summons his sales team into his office for the 'daily motivation meeting'. During these sessions, the sales staff stand and are roundly criticised for their previous day's performance. Not once does Arthur Rowe offer a word of praise; he doesn't believe in it. At the end of these meetings, the sales staff troop out in an even more demotivated state of mind.

Arthur also has the habit of standing behind the sales staff as they try to make appointments by telephone. Again, his only comments are of a critical or sarcastic nature.

Not surprisingly his methods of motivation are major contributors to the large staff turnover among his sales staff.

David's 'Friday injection'
Every Friday afternoon, David Wilson effusively thanks his team for all their efforts during the week. It has become known among the staff as the 'Friday injection' and is no longer taken seriously.

Each week, David holds a staff meeting at which every problem and decision is laid on the table for discussion, although many of the solutions only affect one or two people. The staff find this a time wasting and tedious exercise. As a result, although they like David as a person, his team think he is ineffective as a manager.

Liz takes the trouble

The hotel group for which Liz Cole worked, designed a special weekend package in an attempt to induce additional guests to stay at the hotel during weekends. The promotion was to last for three weeks.

Liz realised that this would mean more work for every member of her team. She wished to maintain the high standard of service for which they were known and so devised a simple scheme which she hoped would motivate everyone. She discussed her ideas with the head receptionist and the head porter, who were in full agreement. Liz persuaded the hotel to fund her scheme. She called a brief staff meeting to explain the promotion and emphasised the need to give good service but refrained from disclosing her scheme.

At the end of the first month, Liz personally thanked each member of her team and gave them a good bottle of wine. She repeated the process at the end of the second month, this time giving them a £15 gift voucher. At the end of the final month, she again thanked everyone and gave them a scarf for the women and a tie for the men.

Without exception, the staff were highly motivated by Liz's gestures and cannot wait for the next promotion.

SUMMARY

Good motivation

- Ascertain the individual's needs.
- Motivate by satisfying individual needs.
- Give praise when due.
- Praise effort as well as results.
- Give unannounced rewards for effort and ideas.
- Regular two-way communication.
- Involve the staff as appropriate.
- Look for signs of demotivation and act immediately.

Bad motivation

- Motivate the team not individuals.
- Use the carrot (incentives).
- Motivate by fear.
- Only praise exceptional results.
- Ignore signs of demotivation.

DISCUSSION POINTS

1. What motivated you to read this book?

2. What are the individual needs of your team?

3. You have recently taken over the management of a new team, none of whom you knew before. One of your staff, Tom, is nearing retirement. His work is of an acceptable standard but no more. You notice that he rarely becomes involved with other members of the team, either in the office or socially. He objects to any criticism of his work, however constructive. He arrives at work on time and leaves at exactly 5.00pm each day, often leaving jobs unfinished. How will you motivate Tom to become a better team member?

5
How to Delegate

SPOKEN FROM EXPERIENCE

'The most difficult thing in the world is to know how to do a thing and to watch somebody else doing it wrong, without comment.' – T H White.

'The surest way for an executive to kill himself is to refuse to learn how, when and to whom to delegate work.' – J C Penny.

'Unless the executive establishes priorities for the things he is to do himself, he will not delegate responsibility properly because he will never know what to delegate.' Professor Ray E Brown.

'It is never a sign of weakness when a man in a high position delegates authority; on the contrary, it is a sign of his strength and of his capacity to deserve success.' – Walter Lippman.

EXCUSES, EXCUSES!

Delegation, like the pathway to hell in *Pilgrim's Progress*, is littered with good intentions. Most people vow that when they become a manager they will become good delegators. However, when they reach the giddy heights of management they too often fail to carry out this promise.

Why is it that so many managers are reluctant to delegate even the simplest of tasks? With few exceptions, the reasons are purely psychological, as illustrated by the following list:

- Assumed lack of ability of subordinates—until you make yourself aware of the strengths and weaknesses of your staff, it is natural to assume that they lack the necessary skills.

- 'It's quicker to do it myself'—in the short term, yes, but not in the long term. If a task takes you one hour each week, you could save yourself forty-five to fifty hours a year by delegating it to someone else.

- The manager enjoys the task—until his recent retirement, the chairman and founder of a haulage company in the south east of England always prepared the holiday schedule for his 230 employees. Despite the attempts of his fellow directors, he could not be persuaded to delegate this comparatively simple task. He enjoyed doing it.

- The manager has always done it—why? Is it not now the time for a change?

- Reluctance to share knowledge—after all, knowledge is power.

- Ego—the manager wants to be considered to be a martyr and to be seen to be overworked.

- Fear—fear that the person who takes on the task, may do it better than the manager; fear that the staff may feel that the task is too demeaning for them; fear of the unknown.

- Over protective of staff—not wishing to appear to be overloading the staff with work.

- Politics—the top management would not approve.

- Lack of communicaton skills—not knowing how to delegate.

- Not knowing what to delegate.

- Having no one to delegate to—lack of staff

Which, if any, of the above are you guilty of and what are you going to do about it? Only the last three in the list are genuine reasons. All but the last can be overcome by improving your skills.

Example
Carol had worked in the administrative department for the past two years and was doing the same tasks now as on the day she started. She was becoming bored and wanted a new challenge.

Recently she had overheard her manager complaining to one of his colleagues that he was overworked and under paid. She thought that the time was right to approach him.

'Excuse me Eric,' Carol began, 'I was wondering if you had any jobs that I could do for you.'

'What's the matter, don't you have enough work?', Eric replied.

'Yes, but I've been doing the same things since I started and it's become routine and repetitive,' she said.

'That's what you're paid for,' Eric responded.

'I know, but I was wondering whether I could take on the monthly production statistics that you do,' Carol asked hopefully.

'No,' Eric said with some annoyance. 'I haven't got the time to show you what to do, anyway it's quicker to do it myself and then I know it will be right.'

With that uncalled for rebuff, Carol returned to her desk, very demotivated. Realising that her future with the company looked bleak, she decided to seek alternative employment.

WHY DELEGATE?

Good delegation will give many benefits to you as the manager and to your staff. Good delegation will provide:

- You with more time in which to manage.
- Valuable development for your staff.
- A means of motivating your staff.
- More staff job satisfaction.
- A sense of responsibility for your staff.
- A good working environment.
- More staff involvement.
- You with more respect from your staff.
- Improved teamwork.

Example

One afternoon, the personnel and training manager of an electronic components company was in his office. He was sitting back in his chair with his eyes closed and his hands steepled under his chin. Apart from a telephone, a blank sheet of paper and a pen, his desk was clear. His office door was open. Walking past the office, the company's chief executive looked in. Seeing the manager apparently asleep, he entered.

'And what do you think you're doing?' the chief executive asked with a tinge of annoyance in his voice.

'Managing,' was the reply.

'Daydreaming more like.' The tone expressed his boss's rising anger.

'Actually, I am considering a suggestion put to me by one of my team for introducing psychometric testing for prospective employees,' the manager explained.

'That's all very well but what about your work?'

'My staff are more than capable of dealing with the day-to-day tasks, taking the necessary decisions within their roles and solving most of the everyday problems. Each morning, I prioritise my tasks, deal with them and so have time to manage.'

'What if something happens that they can't deal with?' the chief executive asked.

'My door is always open and they know that they can come and see me at any time.' the manager replied confidently.

As the chief executive had no complaints about the department he left, realising that there were a few lessons he could learn about delegation from his personnel and training manager.

YOUR DELEGATION CHECKLIST

Read through the following questions and tick yes or no as appropriate to you.

1. Do you have time to plan your work and supervise
    your people properly, in fact to manage?   Yes/No

2. Do you do everything in your power to develop
    the abilities of your staff?   Yes/No

3. Can you carry out all your duties adequately?   Yes/No

4. Could anyone else do part of your work more quickly
    or economically?   Yes/No

5. Is the workload generally shared equally between
    you and your staff?   Yes/No

6. Do you ensure that when you are away from your
    work place the work in your department does not
    suffer as a consequence?   Yes/No

7. Do you have sufficient time to consider and initiate
    improved working methods?   Yes/No

8. Are you good at organising the job to be done and
    leaving the details to the person who is to do it?   Yes/No

9. Do you show your staff that you are confident in
their ability to do a job? Yes/No

10. Do you allow your staff to do a job in their own
particular way? Yes/No

11. Are you constantly checking up on the work carried
out by those under your control? Yes/No

12. Do you have to decide all matters, or can your staff
use their own initiative in taking decisions sometimes? Yes/No

13. Do you set high enough standards for the work you
delegate? Yes/No

14. Are your standards too high? Yes/No

15. Do you find yourself doing the job of one of your
staff when they should be doing it themselves? Yes/No

16. Do you delegate the authority and responsibility, that
goes with the task? Yes/No

17. If things go wrong, has the person, to whom you
delegated, enough information to put things right
on his own initiative? Yes/No

18. Are you often interrupted by your staff asking about
the job you have delegated? Yes/No

19. Do you find that mistakes are often made because
your instructions are not followed? Yes/No

20. Do you always provide correct and adequate training
for the tasks you delegate? Yes/No

You should have answered yes to all of the above except numbers 11, 14, 15, 18 and 19. If you have scored 15 or more correctly, you are well on the way to becoming a good delegator. Less than 15 means that you need to work on this area of your technique.

You have now identified those areas in your delegation skills that require improvement.

HOW TO DELEGATE

Good delegation will be highly motivating to all concerned, while poor delegation will be very demotivating.

To help you to delegate effectively, follow this sequence of simple steps:

- Decide the task to be delegated. Preferably it should be a continuing task, not a 'one-off'.

- Select the most appropriate member of your staff to delegate to. This will largely depend upon the task.

- Check the existing workload of that staff member. You will not be thanked if they think that you are dumping extra work on them. It may be necessary to delegate some of their work to somebody else.

- Discuss your proposals with the person you have selected. Explain the task, its importance and why you have chosen them. Get their agreement to take on the job.

- Train the person until you are both happy that they can do the task. See the section on Training p. 55.

- Establish and agree a monitoring procedure.

- Assign the necessary authority and responsibility with the task.

Points to remember
- The amount of delegation by a manager should be a balance between dictatorship and abdication.

- Accountability should always go with responsibility.

- Let go of the reins when the time is right.

WHAT TO DELEGATE

One of the problems facing managers when it comes to delegation, is knowing what and what not to delegate. As a rule of thumb, you should be able to delegate the following:

- Projects that expand the capabilities of the individual; eg preparation of statistical data, restructuring departmental work flows, recommendations for future activities.
- Complete tasks with responsibilities. Giving only part of a job will provide no sense of achievement.
- Closed decisions with clear cut criteria.

On the other hand, tasks that should not be delegated include:

- Management prerogatives and key tasks; eg salary review, departmental objectives, confidential or sensitive tasks.
- Part tasks with no overall responsibility.
- Only boring, mundane, routine tasks.
- Open, ad hoc decisions.

Example
One day, Maureen went to her manager to ask if she could leave work early on the following Thursday, to visit the hairdresser. She caught him at a bad time. He was in the middle of completing a confidential report.

'Don't both me now,' her manager said 'have a word with Harry.'
Harry was the oldest member of the team.

'Harry,' Maureen said, 'Mike has asked me to see you about my leaving early on Thursday to get my hair done.'

Harry was rather taken aback by this request and after a few moments consideration, said: 'Well, I suppose it will be all right, but make sure that you finish your work first.'

Maureen was highly delighted. The problem was that over the next few weeks, other members of the team went to Harry with similar requests, which he felt obliged to grant.

It was only when Mike noticed that people were no longer asking him for decisions and he was losing control, that he realised the folly of his earlier delegation to Harry.

Which tasks would you delegate?
Read through the following list of tasks and tick those that you could, as a manager, delegate to your staff.

1. The recruitment of a new member of staff.
2. A project in an area in which you are particularly competent.
3. The preparation of forecasts or budgets.
4. Recommendations for future changes.

TRAINING BREAKDOWN SHEET

Activity: How to prepare an invoice

Preparation: Supply of completed order forms; supply of blank invoice sets; customer code list; product code book. Use ball point pen.

STAGES	KEY POINTS
Heading	1. Customer Name and Address (Order Form) 2. Customer Code, if any (Customer Code List). 3. Today's Date
Main Body	For each item: 4. Product detail (Order Form) 5. Quantity (Order Form) 6. Product Code (Product Code Book) 7. Price per item (Product Code Book) 8. Total price per item Qty × Price
Calculations	9. Add total prices – enter in box 1 10. Customer discount if any (Customer Code List) – enter in box 2 11. Deduct Discount from Total – enter in box 3 Discounted Total 12. Calculate 10% Carriage – enter in box 4 13. Add Carriage to Discounted Total – Enter in box 5 14. Calculate VAT @ 17½% – enter in box 6 15. Add VAT to Sub Total – enter in box 7
Checking	16. Tick and sign Order Form. 17. At the end of each day, give Order Forms and completed invoices to Sheila.

Figure 2. Training Breakdown Sheet.

5. Employee disciplinary procedures.
6. Routine work.
7. Developing suggestions for new policies and procedures.
8. Performance appraisal interviews with employees.
9. Coaching or counselling an employee to help him/her improve their performance.
10. Preparation of background reports on complex issues.
11. Dealing with customer complaints.
12. Where to hold the departmental Christmas lunch.

Only 1, 5, 8 and 9 are part of your key tasks and should not be delegated.

HOW TO TRAIN YOUR STAFF

Although training is one of a manager's prime functions, too many managers say that they do not have enough time to train. This excuse is often used to conceal the fact that they do not know how to train. Often this can be overcome by sending people away on training courses. This is fine as far as it goes but is of no help when having to train somebody on a one-to-one basis as, for example, when delegating a task.

Training does take time. However, good training is time well spent. As a manager you should set aside sufficient time to train your staff as required.

Preparing for training

Before attempting to train anyone, it is essential that you prepare correctly. If you have been doing the job for any length of time, you will take short cuts and have certain information stored in your head. Remember, your trainee will not have these advantages and so you need to analyse the task and break it down into stages making sure that you cover every detail. Do not assume that your trainee has any prior knowledge of the job. Leave nothing to chance.

To help you in the preparation, make out a **breakdown sheet** similar to that shown in Figure 2. This names the task, shows the various stages of the job and the key points that you need to emphasise at each stage. This will aid you in ensuring that you have covered every detail, however small, and you can use it as a crib sheet when doing the training. You will only need to make one breakdown sheet for each task as it can be used over and over again.

Arrange with your trainee when the training is to take place and allow sufficient time. If it is a long or complicated task, it will be better to divide the training into two or more, digestible sessions.

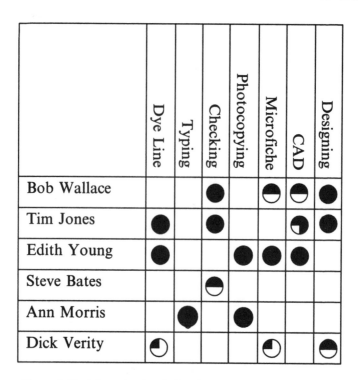

Figure 3. Training plan for design department of medium sized engineering company.

Training

- Prepare yourself. Make sure that there will be no interruptions. Check that you have all the necessary equipment, documentation and so on including your breakdown sheet.
- Prepare the trainee. Re-emphasise the importance of the task and check that the trainee can see everything that you will be doing. Unless machinery is involved, it is ideal if you and the trainee sit side by side.
- Present the instruction. Tell the trainee what you are going to do, then show them whilst talking it through. Present one stage at a time, stress the key points, check their understanding by asking 'Have I made that clear?' Present at a suitable pace for the learner, be patient.
- Practice by the trainee. Ask the trainee to do that stage and tell you what they are doing. If errors occur, don't correct them, point them out and ask the trainee to correct them. Give help as necessary and repeat this step until both of you are satisfied that the trainee can do the task.

Repeat these last two steps for each stage of the task.

- Set trainee to work. Indicate trainee's responsibilities; tell them who can help if you are unavailable, encourage questions and agree monitoring procedures.

Monitoring progress
Meet with your trainee at the agreed time to discuss progress. Encourage and help them as necessary. Never give the impression that you are checking up. Let them carry out the task for themselves and they will come to you for help when they need it. End the monitoring when you are both satisfied that it is no longer necessary.

Drawing up training plans
To help you to decide who to delegate tasks to, and to show you what training is required to ensure adequate cover for all the tasks and duties in your department, prepare a training plan as illustrated in Figure 3.

On the left-hand side of the chart write the name of each team member, including yourself, and along the top each task and duty carried out within your department. Draw a circle for each task done by each individual. Now make an assessment of each person's ability at each task. If you consider them to be 25 percent competent, fill in a quarter of that circle; 50 percent, half; 75 per cent three-quarters; fully competent, fill in the complete circle. This will tell you who needs training in what area. As their abilities increase, you shade in the circles accordingly.

This will take some of your management time to set up, but once operating it is simple to update and will provide you with a very useful management tool.

CASE STUDIES

Arthur's secret fears
Roger Beale, one of Arthur Rowe's salesmen, had survived six months with the company and, despite Arthur's mangement style, had been quite successful in gaining new business. He decided that he wanted more responsibility.

One morning he took the unprecedented step of entering Arthur's office whilst he was in residence.

'Mr Rowe,' Roger began, 'I've been with the company for over six months and during that time have been quite successful in winning new business. I think it is now time that I had more responsibility.'

'What?' Arthur exploded 'You cheeky little blighter. Get out before I throw you out!'

Unperturbed, Roger continued, 'I believe that in recognition of my efforts, I should take over some of the national accounts.'

Regaining his composure, Arthur replied, 'You don't have the know how to deal with any of our major customers. Anyway, that's my province.'

'But surely I could learn,' said Roger.

'It's a matter of experience,' Arthur said. 'I've known them for years. They deal with me, not the company. I suggest you get back to your desk and get on with your work.'

Realising that he could not win, Roger returned disconsolately to his desk.

This brief encounter brought to the surface all of Arthur's fears about delegation. His assumed lack of ability in his salesmen; fear of sharing his knowledge and losing power; his feeling that nobody could deal with the blue chip accounts as well as he could; and his unwillingness to develop his staff.

David is forced to let go

The local authority for which David Wilson worked decided to install a system for monitoring the quality of their home helps. It would be the responsibility of David's department to set up and run that system.

Not wishing to give additional tasks to what he considered to be his overworked staff, David decided to look after the scheme himself. Although it meant that he had to work longer hours, he did not mention it to his team.

A few weeks later, Deirdrie, his most loyal employee, noticed that he was staying late more often than before. When she asked him why, David had no alternative but to tell her about the new system. She was livid. Not because David was becoming overworked but because she and her colleagues were responsible for allocating home helps and she thought that this area of her responsibility was being usurped.

When Deirdrie told her colleagues what David was doing, they virtually forced him to delegate the monitoring to them.

This was a case of a manager being over protective towards his staff.

Liz gets delegating

One of Liz Cole's tasks was to analyse the sources which persuaded clients to stay at the hotel, eg advertising, travel agents, referrals and so on. At present guests were asked to tick the appropriate box on the registration cards, from which Liz prepared her statistics. This was not an ideal system as she had to collect the cards after the guest had left; as often as not, no boxes would be ticked.

She decided to delegate this task to the receptionists. First she discussed it with her head receptionist and they agreed that instead of ticking boxes, the receptionist would ask the guests the question at the time of booking in. Each receptionist would have a sheet on which to record this information. Each Monday morning, these sheets would be collected and a weekly analysis prepared.

Liz decided to ask Barbara to undertake this task. She was a bright girl and had been at the hotel for over a year. Liz discussed the task with Barbara, telling her why it was important and what was involved. A training session took place in Liz's office and it was arranged that either Liz or the head receptionist would discuss the analysis with Barbara for the first three weeks.

Everything appeared to work well, Barbara was happy and another girl was trained to do the task when Barbara was away.

SUMMARY

Good delegation

- Choose the appropriate person.
- Delegate complete tasks.
- Provide full training for the task.
- Ensure both you and the person delegated are satisfied that they can do the job.
- Delegate tasks that will develop the person.
- Arrange to monitor progress.
- Delegate the authority and responsibility along with the task.

Bad delegation

- Giving additional tasks to already overworked staff.
- Delegating only part of a task.
- Nil or inadequate training.
- Constantly checking up on progress.
- Ignoring the person after delegating the task.
- Failing to give the authority or responsibility that goes with the task.
- Delegating too much or too little.

DISCUSSION POINTS

1. Write a list of all those tasks that you do at present, which could be delegated to members of your team.

2. Referring to the Training Plan in Figure 3 on page 56, what additional training is required to ensure adequate cover in cases of holidays and illness?

3. In an attempt to cut costs, your company has dispensed with the services of the contractors who cleaned the offices. It is now the responsibility of each department to keep its own area clean. Each evening all waste paper bins must be emptied at a central point near the car park. Once a week the floor area is to be vacuumed and all desks, cabinets and so on, to be dusted. Equipment will be supplied. How and to whom will you delegate these tasks?

6
How to Build and Lead a Team

SPOKEN FROM EXPERIENCE

'True leadership must be for the benefit of the followers, but the enrichment of the leaders.' – Robert Townsend.

'No amount of study or learning will make a man a leader unless he has the natural qualities of one.' – Sir Archibald Wavell.

'Leadership, like everything else in life that is vital, finds its source in understanding. To be worthy of management responsibility today, a man must have insight into the human heart, for unless he has an awareness of human problems, a sensitivity towards the hopes and aspirations of those whom he supervises, and a capacity for analysis of the emotional forces that motivate their conduct, the projects entrusted to him will not go ahead no matter how often wages are raised.' – Clarence R Randall.

ALL FOR ONE AND ONE FOR ALL

Most people work in groups, whether it be in an office, a laboratory, a hospital, the factory floor or a theatre. Even those who spend much of their working time away from the group, eg salesmen and journalists, contribute to the success of failure of the group by their individual efforts.

Members of sports teams, commercial airliner crews and boards of directors must be aware of the duties and responsibilities of each member of the group, in order that they can achieve their respective objectives. Therefore they must work as a team.

It is equally important that all work groups operate as teams to maximise their efficiency. Whether or not a group becomes a team. depends largely on how they are led.

YOUR SUCCESSFUL TEAM

An analysis of any successful teams will show that they have the following features in common.

- Members share a strong sense of **common purpose**—the hospital operating theatre team have the common purpose of curing the patient.

- Members of the team **interact** to achieve their purpose—players in a soccer team interact by passing the ball to one another, positioning themselves to receive passes and backing up their team mates.

- Each member has a strong sense of the team's **identity**—each member of a tele-sales department is aware that their team is responsible for generating business for their company.

- The team is **small enough** to be self-coordinating. Six is the optimum number of people that can be managed effectively by one person. Thus with few exceptions, successful teams rarely exceed eight. Even a rugby union team divides itself into two groups, eight forwards and seven backs.

- The team has its own internal **code of behaviour**—this may vary from a non-smoking rule in the office, to helping one another without having to ask.

- Members afford each other a high level of **mutual support**—if one person is overloaded with work, the others will 'muck in' and help.

- The team has an **internal structure**—members of a team will assume certain roles according to their likes and abilities.

Are these features apparent in your team? If so, how are they demonstrated?

Successful teams will also carry out these group functions:

- Proposing tasks or goals; defining group problems.
- Requesting facts and relevant information about group concerns; asking for ideas and opinions.
- Providing information; suggesting ideas and opinions.
- Interpreting and reflecting ideas and suggestions; clearing up confusions; giving alternatives.

- Summarising ideas and suggestions; offering decisions or conclusions for the group to accept or reject.
- Checking to see how much agreement has been reached.

These take place without the intervention of the manager.

IDENTIFYING TEAM ROLES

Members of any group will take on specific roles. Extensive research by Dr Melville Belbin at the Henley Management College has identified the following roles:

The natural leader
Not always the formal leader; main concern is for effective teamwork; clarifies the team's aims and objectives; knows the members' strengths and weaknesses; establishes work boundaries and communication channels; is extrovert and calm; dominant but not domineering; possesses common sense rather than high intelligence; exerts authority in a relaxed, unaggressive manner.

Action man/woman
Concerned for action and results; extrovert, impulsive and impatient; confident but easily frustrated; dominant, competitive and quick to offer or accept a challenge; intolerant of woolly thinking; often arrogant or abrasive; may make the team uncomfortable but makes things happen.

Ideas man/woman
Concerned for major issues and fundamentals; provides original suggestions and proposals but may miss details and make mistakes; introvert yet thrustful and uninhibited; dominant and highly-strung; criticises others' ideas and may sulk if own ideas are not accepted; may require judicious flattery and careful handling to get the best from such a person.

Contact man/woman
Concerned with exploring possibilities outside the team; lacks original ideas but encourages innovation; good improviser but can waste time on irrelevancies; extrovert, sociable, gregarious and dominant; often fails to follow things through; easily becomes bored, demoralized and ineffective.

Practical organiser
Turns decisions and strategies into defined tasks that people can deal with; likes to make schedules and charts; needs settled plans and can flounder in uncertain or rapidly changing situations; controlled and calm; has integrity and disciplined approach; efficient and methodical but can be inflexible; can be negative and unconstructive to others' ideas.

Checker
A compulsive meeter of deadlines; needs to check every detail; can get bogged down in detail and lose sight of the objective; greatest asset is the ability to follow through; introvert, anxious, obsessive and impatient; keeps team aware of the need for urgency and attention to detail.

Judge
The most objective, uninvolved member; provides dispassionate analysis; likes time to consider; introvert and lacks warmth and spontaneity; low enthusiasm but calm and dependable; although fairminded and open to change is often negative and unreceptive; may be tactless and disparaging which can lower team morale.

Team worker
Concerned for team unity and good spirits; although contribution is not always visible, when pressure threatens to disrupt the team, his loyalty and support are invaluable; extrovert and calm; soft and indecisive; likeable and a good listener; builds on the ideas of others; dislikes confrontation and tries to avoid or defuse it.

Which of the above roles are apparent in your team? Which do you wish to encourage?

HOW YOU CAN BUILD AN EFFECTIVE TEAM

Ideally a manager should be able to select the people with whom he wishes to work and so have a team suitable for the situation. Few of us enjoy such a luxury. You, in common with 99.9 percent of managers, probably inherited a group of people with whom to work. You may be fortunate in that they are already working as an efficient and successful team. If that is the case, leave well alone. If not, the following suggestions will help you to build a team to suit your needs.

Techniques you can use
- Make yourself aware of the strengths and limitations of each member. This will help you to identify areas that need to be developed.
- Ensure that everyone understands and accepts the task or objective. Discussion of the objective should be such that team members can commit themselves to it.
- Encourage participation in agreeing objectives and targets. Targets that are thrust upon people can be very demotivating and are hardly likely to get commitment to achieving them.
- Let each member of the team know what you expect them to achieve and the standards to be attained.
- Try to group related tasks so that the team know that they can make their jobs easier by cooperating with others.
- Where possible, rotate jobs so that your staff identify with the team and not just their own tasks.
- Ensure that communication flows freely between the team members.
- Encourage informal meetings to resolve problems.
- Discourage cliques and factions from developing in the team. They will have a detrimental effect on team work.
- Your actions should demonstrate that, although you are the manager, you are very much part of the team. Non-playing captains rarely have much positive influence on team building.

Don't expect immediate success. Building a successful team can be a slow process and requires patience and perseverance on your part. If things do not work the first time, don't blame the team, try again, you will get it together eventually.

Example
A group of workers were engaged in assembling electronic navigation equipment. Each person had their own specific task and each morning would come in, sit at their defined work place, carry out their job and then go home. The only real communication was idle chat to relieve the boredom.

Each person was paid on piecework. If there was a hold-up on the production line due to either a slow worker or a lack of components, arguments would break out as other peoples' wages would be affected. In such cases the supervisors had to intervene and sort out the problem.

Any stranger entering the assembly shop, would be confronted by twenty-two demotivated, bored individuals who had very little interest in what they were doing. There was certainly no evidence that they were a team.

As far as Peter Moore, the manager, was conerned the workers were only there for the money. He was not concerned that there was a high turnover of people as long as the job was done.

Following Mr Moore's retirement a new manager, Paul Rogers, was appointed from outside the company. It did not take him long to note the degree to which the workforce had become demoralised and determine to do something about it.

Calling the group together, he asked them to let him know what problems they had relating to their work. These ranged from complaints about the canteen to a slow supply of parts.

Paul listed those problems that he and the group could do something about and asked them for their ideas. Not surprisingly most of the suggestions were about better lighting, seating and sacking the storeman. When Paul asked whether they would like to do other jobs, the idea was greeted with suspicion. The group thought that it would mean more work. However, the manager said that the assembly work could be divided into sections and each person trained to perform all of the tasks in one section. They would spend two weeks on one type of task before moving on to another job for two weeks. He explained that this would give them variety in their work, help them to understand each other's work problems, encourage them to improve the quality of their work and so lose less piecework money because of rejects.

Although it took some three months to get the new system up and running, the result was that most problems were solved by the workers themselves. They talked to each other about work and the product. They set themselves targets and everyone felt involved. The group of individuals had become a team.

UNDERSTANDING LEADERSHIP

Are leaders born or made? To paraphrase a comment supposedly made by a master at Eton College, 'Johnson minor is not a born leader, *yet!*'

People become leaders by:

- **Election** by their peers; political leaders, for example.
- The **situation** which suits their personality, ability or knowledge; Gandi, Churchill, Napoleon, Hitler come into this category.
- **Appointment**; such as promotion into a management post.

Unfortunately, many of those appointed are leaders in name only. Good managers and good leaders are synonymous. It is very difficult to become a good manager without being at least a competent leader.

Your personal leadership checklist
Below are some statements about leadership. Out of each pair tick the one which applies to 'leader' (as you understand the word).

1. (a) The leader trusts his subordinates. ____
    (b) Subordinates must prove that they can be trusted. ____

2. (a) You should delegate authority wherever possible. ____
    (b) As a leader you need to demonstrate your position even if you have to interfere with your subordinates' work. ____

3. (a) A leader exercises power through people. ____
    (b) To survive, a leader must exercise power over people. ____

4. (a) I believe that credit should accrue to the department and to me as its head. ____
    (b) I always give credit where it is due. ____

5. (a) When I give instructions to be carried out, I always give the reasons behind them. ____
    (b) There are times when a leader must give orders without an explanation. ____

6. (a) A good leader needs to be obeyed. ____
    (b) A good leader inspires loyalty and initiative. ____

7. (a) Leadership is about managing the people or the task. ____
    (b) Leadership is about managing people and the task. ____

8. (a) To be a good leader you must lead by example. ____
    (b) To be a good leader you must inspire people. ____

9. (a) A good leader demands respect by his position. ____
    (b) A good leader earns respect by his conduct. ____

10. (a) Good leaders are always in the thick of the action. ____
    (b) It is necessary to stand back and ensure that those you are leading are doing the right things. ____

The correct answers are: 1a, 2a, 3a, 4b, 5a, 6b, 7b, 8b, 9b, 10b. Seven or more correct answers suggests that you are on the right lines. Less than seven, beware of confusing leadership with dictatorship.

Qualities of leadership

As suggested in the quotation by Sir Archibald Wavell, no amount of study will make you a leader; there must be some in-born qualities that can be developed. Many people have such qualities but lack the chance to explore or develop them.

The qualities of the effective leader in a modern business setting are:

- Personal integrity—complete and pervasive.

- Intelligence and knowledge—intelligence towards people and knowledge of the task with the ability to communicate with your group.

- Empathy—knowing that the job is done through others—always striving to know them better—trying to preserve and develop human dignity.

- Self-awareness—the good leader has a powerful urge that impels him or her to get things done, to organise and to take responsibility.

- Emotional security—emotionally balanced enough not to be crushed by defeat or over-elated by success. Aware of his or her hostilities and prejudices while trying to keep them to a minimum. Never afraid of new ideas that might threaten status—a manager under stress tends to drive, not lead.

Who creates the right leadership climate?

- The manager who really listens and encourages.
- The manager who wants to improve conditions.
- The manager who encourages involvement in all areas.
- The manager who encourages his team to be self-reliant.
- The manager who ensures that everyone is aware of their responsibilities.

What does the best leader recognise?

- That his position never gives him the right to command.
- That he has a duty never to humiliate people.

- That when the job is done, the people who did it for him will say that they did it for themselves.

Your role as a leader

Demands of leadership
The three demands of a leader as described by John Adair are:

- Task needs—to get the job done.
- Group needs—to build and maintain team spirit.
- Individual needs—to harmonise the needs of the individual within the needs of the task and the group.

These needs overlap and impinge upon one another. A change in one will affect the other two. For example, if the task changes, say targets are increased by 10 percent, this will affect the morale of the team and put more pressure on each individual, particularly the weaker ones. The leader must therefore take action to prevent the morale from dropping and to encourage and help the individuals.

The duties of a leader

- Gain the commitment and cooperation of the team.
- Get the group into action to achieve agreed objectives.
- Make the best use of the skills, talents and energies of the team.
- Eliminate uncertainty.
- Coordinate effort.
- Resolve individual and group needs.
- Build group synergy.
- Balance internal and external needs.
- Represent the group to other groups.

Leadership styles
Of the several ways of analysing leadership styles, one of the best and most relevent to the business manager, is the analysis of behaviour in leadership situations. One of the most significant, identified by Robert Tannenbaum and Warren Schmidt, is the way decisions are reached in working groups. Their continuum, illustrated in Figure 4, shows six different styles which depend upon the relative influence of the manager and the group.

Telling—the manager makes a decision and tells his group what to do. The group have no say in the matter. 'We have to reduce costs by 15 percent. I want you to keep all telephone calls to the afternoon, only use second-class post and write on both sides of every sheet of paper.'

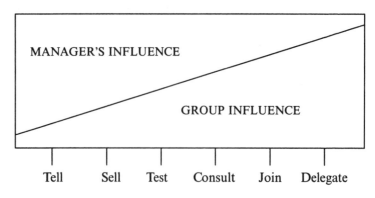

Figure 4. Six styles of making management decisions
(Identified by Tannenbaum and Schmidt).

Selling—the manager makes a decision and tries to persuade the group to accept it by letting them know the benefits. 'In order to keep the company viable and prevent any redundancies, we need to reduce costs by 15 percent. I would like you to only make telephone calls in the afternoon and use second-class postage.'

Testing—the manager proposes his solution and asks the group for their reactions. 'To help cut costs by 15 percent, I suggest that we make our phone calls in the afternoon and use second-class post. Do you agree?'

Consulting—the manager presents the problem to the group, puts forward his solution and asks for contributions from the group. 'We must cut costs by 15 percent. I suggest that we make telephone calls only in the afternoon and use second-class post. Do you agree and what other cost-saving ideas do you have?'

Joining—the manager states the problem and asks the group for solutions which will be accepted provided that they do not contravene company policy. 'We have to cut costs by 15 percent. Let's discuss the matter and see what ideas we can come up with to achieve this.'

Delegating—the manager leaves the group to find a solution without any input from him. 'Let me know what we can do to cut costs by 15 percent. We'll meet on Monday to see what ideas you have.'

Influences on management style
There are three things which affect the style used. They are the manager, the subordinates and the situation.

The manager
  - how strongly he/she feels that they must demonstrate that they are the boss.

- how much trust he/she has in their staff.
- leadership inclinations; by nature, some managers are autocratic, other democratic.
- how secure a manager feels in uncertain situations; the more control you give to the staff, the less control you have on the outcome.

The subordinate
- readiness to assume responsibility for decision-making.
- relevant knowledge and experience.
- interest in the problem.
- some people prefer clear cut decisions, other prefer a wide degree of freedom.

The situation
- the type of organisation; some demand autocratic behaviour, others are more permissive.
- the problem; some can only be solved by one person, the manager.
- time constraint; time pressure may make it difficult to consult with anyone.

No doubt you will have your preferred style of management. However, good leadership is about being flexible and using the most appropriate style for the situation and the people concerned.

MANAGING DIFFERENT PEOPLE

The function of a manager is to lead, motivate and develop the team to achieve agreed objectives. However, every team is made up of a number of individuals with varying degrees of knowledge and experience, so let us first consider the techniques to apply in managing people in different situations.

Managing inexperienced new recruits

Young people who have recently left full time education and have little in the way of work experience will be entering a world that is both new and strange to them. Initially they will respond best to a tell/sell style of management. Ensure that they receive a comprehensive **induction training** which should include information about the company, its products or services and the market, the functions of the department and full training for their job.

Where practical, assign one of your more experienced staff members to act as their **mentor**. Someone who can help them to adjust and settle into the work environment.

For the first four to six weeks arrange an informal interview with the new recruit each Friday, to review their progress and to identify any problems or difficulties that they may have.

Managing graduates
These can be handled in a similar way to other inexperienced new staff. However, because of their graduate status, they are very likely to expect special attention and quick promotion. It is essential not to give them preferential treatment as this could lead to ill feeling among your established team. Concentrate on their abilities to do the job, rather than on their education. They may believe that they are a cut above the rest, so the weekly interview can also be used to help them become a member of the team.

Managing experienced new recruits
After the initial induction and job training, use their past work experience to get them involved as quickly as possible. Such people are likely to respond more positively to a join/consult management style.

Managing those approaching retirement
Some people really look forward to their retirement because they have planned how they will use their time positively. Others will be dreading it because they only see a reduction in their income and have a fear of no longer being 'wanted'.

Those in the first category are unlikely to cause you many problems. Continue to use their experience and skills for the benefit of the team. Show a genuine interest in their plans for the future.

People in the second group are likely to become increasingly demotivated. As their manager, you will need to counsel them to persuade them to think and plan positively for the future. You may need to suggest, through third party reference, that they visit a retirement counsellor or attend one of the many external seminars dealing with retirement. Do not allow their negative feelings to fester as it will eventually affect other members of your team.

Managing redundancy
Should you be in the unenviable position of having to make one of your team redundant, counsel them about their future. Seek outside help if you do not feel capable of handling this situation. It is vital that you allay any fears among the rest of your team with regular open communication. Do not be afraid to discuss the situation with them.

Managing 'difficult' people

One of the questions on most manager's lips is 'How do I deal with difficult people?' The first response is, 'What do you mean by difficult?' They usually mean people who do not conform to accepted standards because they are uncooperative, constant complainers, aggressive and so on.

The second question is, 'What is the cause of this unsocial behaviour?' Use counselling techniques to discover the core reason and help them to find a solution. If this does not work, employ the **behavioural change** techniques described in Chapter 7.

CASE STUDIES

Arthur cracks the whip

Arthur Rowe's sales director had told him that revenue must be increased by 10 percent the next year. He expected this to be achieved by the sales department. Arthur called a meeting of his salesmen.

'We need to increase revenue by 12½ percent over the next twelve months. To achieve this I want you to make more appointments and convert more of them into orders. From now on there will be no discounts for first orders. I want you to contact all your customers and tell them that their discount will be cut by 5 percent until further notice. Right, off you go and get on with it.'

The salesmen left the meeting feeling that a difficult job had been made even harder and complaining that they had had no say in the matter.

David 'shares the problem'

In the light of recent publicity, David Wilson's employers had told him that they wanted his department to help to prevent possible child abuse in their area.

At a meeting of his staff, David put the problem to the group.

'I really don't know what we can do about this. Perhaps you can give it some thought and we'll have a meeting next week and see what ideas you have.'

'But some of us aren't involved with children,' said Alison, one of his team.

'Yes I know,' replied David 'But if you can come up with anything it will be most helpful.'

The group had too much work to give this possible problem any real thought. As a result, nothing of real value emerged from the next meeting.

Liz suggests an agenda

The hotel group for which Liz Cole worked, decided that it was time for a change of uniform for the porters. Liz called a meeting of the porters.

'The hotel have decided that we need to improve your uniform and give them a more modern look. As this affects you directly, I would like to discuss it with you. We need to consider colour, style and practicability. Provided it is not too outlandish, I'm sure that whatever we come up with will be accepted.'

A lively discussion followed and a new uniform was agreed. The porters were happy and commited to wearing it as they had had a major say in the design.

SUMMARY

Good leadership practices

- Change your style to suit the situation.
- Be aware of the strengths and limitations of your staff.
- Encourage staff involvement in all appropriate areas.
- Make sure that everyone knows what they are supposed to do.
- Be supportive.
- Ensure that everyone knows what is expected of them.
- Be a member of the team as well as its leader.
- Encourage and listen to ideas and suggestions.
- Be aware of the needs of the task, the group and the individuals.

Bad leadership practices

- Make sure everyone knows who is the boss.
- Rule with an iron hand.
- Choose a management style and stick with it.
- Give too much authority.
- Reach the objective regardless of the people.
- Ensure that your staff are happy, even if the task is not always completed.

DISCUSSION POINTS

1. What management styles have been used in the above case studies? What would be the most appropriate in the circumstances?

2. Give examples of appropriate situations for each of the styles of management.

3. Analyse the preferred styles used by your fellow managers.

7
How to Make Good Decisions

SPOKEN FROM EXPERIENCE

'The most common source of mistakes in management decisions is the emphasis on finding the right answer rather than the right question.' – Peter F Drucker

'A decision is what a man makes when he can't get anyone to serve on a committee.' – Fletcher Knebel.

'Decisions, ideas and directives lost much of their usefulness and vigour because of delay.' – E J Thomas.

DECISIONS, DECISIONS

Life is full of decisions. Every day we make decisions, some small others large. Most of these decisions affect only ourselves or our families and many of them are made on experience.

As a manager, you will be expected to make decisions on a wide range of topics and on behalf of people, some of whom will be unknown to you.

The most important point to remember about making decisions, is to *make* one. Prevarication is the enemy of the decision-maker. One of the main reasons why people delay making decisions is the fear of making a mistake. Don't worry about that as long as you learn from any mistakes you make. A recent survey showed that of the decisions made by senior managers in the United Kingdom, only 55 percent proved to be right.

TYPES OF DECISIONS

Managers need to make three types of decisions whilst at work.

- Decisions about work, eg how can we cope with the workload? How should I allocate my resources? How can I get better results from my staff?

- Decisions about people, eg how much time should I spend finding out about my people? What should I delegate and to whom? How can I help my staff to achieve more?

- Decisions about money, eg are we wasting money trying to achieve the impossible? Where can savings be made? How can we reduce wastage?

MANAGING THE DECISION-MAKING PROCESS

All decisions contain a degree of uncertainty, otherwise there would be no decision to make. To help overcome these uncertainties, we can apply the following steps:

- Define the aim—clarify the reasons and objectives.
- Collect the facts—obtain as much information as possible, relevant to the decision.
- Examine the options—study a number of possible options, don't rely solely on past experience.
- Consider the outcome—look at the risk factor of each option and the consequences of a wrong decision.
- Select the best option—decide upon the option with the lowest risk factor which will still meet the aim.
- Do it—once a decision has been reached, put it into action, don't prevaricate.
- Evaluate the decision—assess the eventual result whether it proved to be right or wrong. This information can be used for future decisions.

Comparing the criteria

When comparing the different options, you will need to take account of the various criteria involved; cost, time, complexity, convenience, comfort and so on. As some criteria will be more important than others, they should be suitably weighted and then compared one with another.

Example
Let us assume that you have been asked to represent our company at an important meeting in Paris at 10.30 am next Thursday. You must decide the best way of getting there on time.

You have discovered that there are various methods that you could use and the criteria to be considered are cost, time, comfort and convenience. The possible modes of travel are air, train or car. With the last two you could either travel overnight, or on Wednesday and spend the night in a hotel in Paris.

Air is the most expensive, the quickest and reasonably comfortable. However, it is not very convenient as you have to get to Heathrow and then from Charles de Gaulle airport to the centre of Paris.

Car is the slowest method and the cheapest. It is convenient and reasonably comfortable, however. More so if combined with an overnight stay in Paris.

Train proves to be second quickest. It is more expensive than the car but cheaper than air travel. Also it is reasonably convenient as it is only necessary to get to and from the main line stations in London and Paris and certainly the most comfortable, especially if linked with a stay in Paris.

The most important criteria are that you arrive at the meeting on time, feeling fresh and relaxed. Which method would you choose?

Delegating your decisions

Even as a manager, it should not be necessary to make every decision concerning your staff and work. You can delegate those decisions where a member of your team is:

- better informed of the facts than you,
- more skilled,
- closer to the action,
- the only one to be affected by the decision.

For example, if the office is to be redecorated and there is a choice of colours, let your staff choose them.

Analysing the risk

Whichever option you choose, it is necessary to analyse the risk. Consider the following:

- The likelihood of it going wrong.
- The seriousness of the consequences if it does.

Analyse whether the risk in each of the above will be high, medium or low. Prepare a simple grid as below and tick as appropriate.

	The chance of it going wrong	The seriousness of the consequences
High		
Medium		
Low		

In most cases, if a tick appears in the high row, do not take the risk. Apply this to your choice of travelling to the meeting in Paris.

Giving your decisions

When you are asked for a decision which you cannot delegate, take note of the following points:

- Give your decision as quickly as possible.

- If you need to obtain more details before giving a decision, tell the person concerned and let them know when you will be able to make a decision.

- Always give the reasons for your decision, especially if it is not the one expected.

CASE STUDIES

Arthur's ivory tower

Arthur Rowe has a reputation for giving quick decisions. More often than not, he does not bother to collect the facts but simply says 'No'.

The sales staff soon learned the result of asking their manager for a decision and therefore usually made their own decisions. If the matter involved another department such as accounts or stores, they would ask the manager concerned for a decision. Rather than ask for time off, they took a day's sick leave.

Although Arthur Rowe believed that he had his finger on the pulse, in truth, he was often unaware of what was actually happening in the sales department.

David and the private office

As we have seen, David Wilson was a great believer in the total involvement of his staff. This included most of the decisions that had to be made.

One day David was asked by his boss whether he would like an office of his own, mainly so that he could conduct interviews in private. Obviously this was a decision that David should have made. However, he put it to his team at their next meeting. They put forward all the pros and cons from their point of view. The main outcome being that they each wanted their own offices. This left David even more confused and so as not to upset his staff, he finally decided not to have his own office.

This was a surprise to his boss who overturned the decision and arranged for an office to be constructed. As a result, David had to spend much of his time pacifying his team and even agreed that they could take it in turns to use his office to interview clients.

Liz saves the situation

Liz Cole's staff were well aware of what decisions they could make without referring them to her. When Liz was called upon to make a decision, she made a point of gathering as much data as possible before making it.

One evening, a couple arrived at the hotel stating that they had made a reservation for two nights through their local travel agent. The receptionist was unable to find any record of the booking. As the hotel was full, she was unable to offer them any accommodation. Naturally the two visitors were extremely angry. The receptionist asked Liz for her help. Having been appraised of the situation, Liz asked for more details about the booking. The couple appeared to be bona fide and in order to maintain the hotel's good reputation, Liz decided to offer the couple alternative accommodation at a nearby hotel, plus a complimentary weekend at her own hotel.

These decisions, which only Liz could make, avoided an unpleasant situation and ensured two very satisfied future clients.

SUMMARY

Good decision-making practices
- Make a decision.
- Don't make rash decisions.
- Collect the relevant facts.
- Don't rely entirely on experience.
- Consider several options.
- Analyse the risks.
- Explain the reasons for your decisions.
- Delegate decisions where appropriate.

Bad decision-making practices
- Prevarication.
- Making all decisions concerning your staff.
- Making decisions too quickly.
- Delegating inappropriate decisions.
- Failing to give reasons for decisions.

DISCUSSION POINTS

1. Which decisions could be made by your staff?

2. Under what conditions could you take a high risk decision?

3. Evaluate the results of three major decisions that you have recently taken, relating to your work.

8
How to Manage Problems

SPOKEN FROM EXPERIENCE

'More people spend more time and energy in going around problems than in trying to solve them' – Henry Ford.

'I have yet to see any problem, however complicated, which, when you look at it the right way, did not become still more complicated' – Poul Anderson.

'Many a problem will solve itself if you'll forget it and go fishing' – Olin Miller.

IS THIS MY PROBLEM?

Managers continually face problems in two distinct categories. Those related to the work itself and those related to people. Whilst the objective in both cases is to solve the problem, they are tackled in quite different ways.

When confronted with a problem, the first question to ask yourself is, 'Is this my problem?' If not, then should you really be trying to solve it? However, should the problem be yours and you are the best person to find a solution, make sure that you understand exactly what the problem is. Much time and effort is spent in business trying to solve the wrong problem.

ADDRESSING WORK PROBLEMS

These can be short, medium or long term. Some are simple, others more complex. Many work-related problems can be solved by you alone, whilst others are better served by involving different people. Whatever the problem, it is good practice to have a clearly defined method of handling it.

Taking a systematic approach
How often do we rush into finding a solution to a problem without

spending any time planning what to do? Sometimes we can get away with it, but often as not we will miss or forget a vital point and end up with an incomplete answer. The systematic approach consists of a series of steps that need to be taken and questions that require answers before attempting to find a solution.

Step 1—Analyse
Objective –   What do we wish to achieve?
Reasons –   Why solve the problem?
                     What is is for?
                     Who is it for?
Measurement – How will we determine success or failure?

Step 2—Plan
What needs to be done?
What information do we need?
Who will do what, when and how?

Step 3—Execute
Do it.

Step 4—Evaluate
Review the result.
Analyse successes and failures.
Assess changes for the future.

Although in some cases it may prove difficult, nevertheless it is very important to provide a measurement against which you can evaluate the outcome. Such measures can include cost, profit, dates and response. All measures should be quantifiable to be of any value. Subjective ones are too easy to manipulate. Remember it is as important to evaluate your successes and failures. Vital lessons can be learned from both.

The systematic approach is most appropriate for medium and long term, fairly complex problems.

Example
Your department has been asked to organise an exhibition of your company's products in a local hotel. You have been given a budget and suitable dates.

Step 1
 • Objective: to increase sales of products to local businesses.

- Reasons.
    Why? to make local business more aware of your
    company's product range.
    What? To increase sales revenue.
    Who? The sales department.

- Measurement
    The exhibition takes place on time.
    A minimum of twenty local businesses attend.

Step 2
- What needs to be done?
    Arrange a suitable venue.
    Organise product display.
    Publicity and promotion.
    Supplies of sales literature.
    Get people to man the exhibition.

- What information do we require?
    Availability and costs of a room from local hotels.
    Names and addresses of people to be invited.
    What products will be exhibited.
    Which company personnel will be available.

- Who will do what, when and how?
    Ask for volunteers for the various tasks and delegate
    where necessary.

Step 3
- Hold the exhibition.

Step 4
- Evaluate the results against the measurement criteria. Use this
    information when planning further exhibitions or similar events.

Types of problems
Different types of problem will require different approaches to solving
them. The following can be combined with the systematic approach.

Creative problems
These are the problems for which you are seeking a new or innovative
solution. For example, new ways of promoting your business, new

work methods, where to go for the company annual outing. The most suitable method for solving such problems is by brainstorming. This is a means of generating a large number of ideas from a group of people. The technique is dealt with in detail in Chapter 10.

Changing the status quo
If, for example, you wished to increase the number of staff in your department or reduce the amount of paperwork, a good technique to employ is force field analysis.

List the driving forces, ie the reasons why the change should take place, followed by reasons why it has not happened, restraining forces. These forces can be illustrated in diagrammatic form as shown in Figure 5.

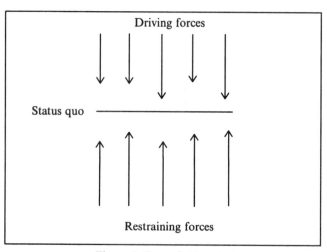

Figure 5. Force field analysis.

The next step is to try and reduce the restraining forces, for it is only then that you will be able to change the status quo.

Example
Problem
    to introduce flexi-time into your department.
Driving forces
    department can be open between 8.00 am and 6.00 pm,
    overseas clients can be more easily contacted during working hours,
    staff will have choice of work times,
    staff will be given more responsibility,

no extra costs involved.
Restraining forces
    how other departments will react,
    less control over staff movements,
    adequate staff cover at all times.

Which of these restraining forces will cause the biggest stumbling block for the scheme?

Logistical problems
These are the ones associated with putting an idea or system into effect. One method of solving such problems is **brainwriting**.

This method requires four to six people, who have some knowledge or experience of the problem, sitting round a table and writing down their solutions. After say ten minutes, the papers are passed to the person on their right, who then reads the solution in front of them and builds upon it. This continues until each person has contributed to every original solution. Then the chairman reads out the suggested solutions, which are evaluated by the group and one is agreed upon. The main benefit of this method is that it forces people to consider and add to solutions other than their own.

Mapping

When you are asked to address a meeting, give a talk or undertake an interview, among the problems you are faced with is what to say and in what order to say it.

You will have selected or been given the subject of your talk. Traditionally, you will sit down with a sheet of paper and a pencil and list the topics that you wish to include. This is the logical approach but will be of no help in ensuring that you cover all the points you wish to make.

A more creative approach is by **mapping**. Firstly write down the subject or title in the centre of your paper and draw a line round it. From this, draw a number of radiating lines, one for each of the major points you wish to include. Identify them by writing one or two words on each line. You can expand these by drawing branches from the main lines, again noting each one.

Being a diagram and thus in no specific order, it will help you to add information as and where required. A further advantage is that it does not have to be completed at one sitting.

Example

You have been asked to make a presentation to your Board, reviewing your department during the past financial year. Your map may look something like the one in Figure 6.

Figure 6. An example of mapping.

ADDRESSING PEOPLE PROBLEMS

As a manager, you will soon discover that most of your problems are caused by people and not only those for whom you are directly responsible. It is important to remember that those people who cause you problems are not always aware of it. If, for example, you are the manager of the purchasing department and people wait until they are out of stock before telling you, this will give you problems when re-ordering.

Similarly, those involved do not necessarily have a problem themselves. Perhaps one of your staff is continually late arriving for work in the morning. Whilst this gives you and your team a problem, the person concerned doesn't seem to have one!

There are three main ways of solving people related problems. The first is to discover the cause of the problem and help the person to solve it for themselves. The second is to discover the cause and deal with it yourself. The third is to change the person's behaviour.

External problems

When a member of your team is causing a problem by arriving late, being absent and so on, you need to discover the reason for it. You will need to talk to the person concerned to find this out. If the reason is due to external factors such as a change in domestic circumstances or an alteration to the train times, your task is to help the person to solve that problem for themselves. You cannot do it for them. Once a viable solution has been found, this should also solve the problem affecting you. The technique for conducting such interviews is dealt with in detail in Chapter 11.

Internal problems

After talking to the person, you may learn that the reason for their behaviour is that they are demotivated for one of the reasons discussed in Chapter 4. If so, it is your job as manager to solve the problem in the right way.

Changing behaviour

This is most appropriate where a person's behaviour damages their performance and/or is affecting other peoples' performance. It can be used when you have been unable to reveal the real reason for their negative behaviour.

Unlike attitudes and feelings which are covert, behaviour is overt. It can be observed, eg shouting, crying, silence. Behaviour is triggered by specific events such as overwork and other peoples' actions. The third element is the benefit that the person receives from their behaviour.

$$\text{Trigger} \longrightarrow \text{Behaviour} \longrightarrow \text{Benefit}$$
$$\text{(event)} \qquad \text{(reaction)} \qquad \text{(gratification)}$$

The objective is to change the negative behaviour to a positive one, not simply to stop the unacceptable behaviour. Only one type of behaviour can be dealt with at a time and there is no attempt to change attitudes or feelings. For example, a baby is hungry (event), it cries (behaviour) and then it is fed (benefit).

How to change behaviour
- Isolate the behaviour to be changed.
- Analyse the event which triggers the behaviour.
- Determine the benefit received from this behaviour.
- Decide what behaviour should replace the existing one.
- Discover the trigger which will result in the new behaviour.
- Provide a positive benefit for the new behaviour.

Example
Every Friday morning Dora, an accounts clerk, received copies of the weeks' invoices. Her task was to sort them into geographical areas and provide totals for each area. On average there were 200 invoices each week.

Dora was not a quick worker; she spent much of her time chatting to her work mates and was always well behind with her work. As 5.00pm approached each Friday, she began to panic and complained loudly about being overworked, often resorting to tears. The result was that her colleagues rallied round to help her finish on time. This meant that they did not always complete their own work on time.

Dora's manager decided to change her behaviour. She began by analysing the situation:

1. Trigger—having 200 invoices to analyse on Friday.
2. Behaviour—panic, complaining and tears.
3. Benefit—help from her colleagues.

The manager realised that she had to change the trigger. Instead of waiting until Friday to give Dora the invoices, she arranged for her to receive them at the end of each day during the week, so that she could analyse them on a daily basis. As a result, Dora no longer had any reason to panic or complain and completed the task on time without any help from others.

Other points to remember when changing people's behaviour are:

- It is better to reward the 'right' behaviour than to punish the 'wrong' one.
- Short-term benefits are better than long-term ones.
- If it is not possible to change the trigger, withhold the benefit from the negative behaviour and restore it when the behaviour changes.
- Only individual behaviour can be changed, not that of people 'en masse'.

There are limitations to this method:
- It only deals with one behaviour at a time.
- It is not an immediate solution.
- It deals with the symptoms, not the causes.

If the problem is caused by people outside your direct control, talk to them. Tell them about the problem and the results. Suggest what they could do to alleviate the situation. This can often be enough to solve the problem.

CASE STUDIES

Arthur demands more aggression

Arthur Rowe favoured the 'confrontational' approach to solving problems, particulatly those relating to people. Recently two new competitors had entered the field with better and less expensive systems than those produced by Arthur's company. As a result, his company was losing business.

He called his sales team together for an extra meeting.

'Right, gentlemen.' he began. 'As you know DPM and Lockyers are now selling against us and taking away a lot of our business. This is causing me a problem. We must be more aggressive.' The salesmen sat in silence, knowing that a solution was about to be provided.

'Instead of telephoning, I want you out there cold calling, at least twenty calls each per day. If this doesn't bring in more sales, I'll want to know the reason why.'

The salesmen dispersed, completely unprepared and untrained for their new role. Not surprisingly, business did not improve.

Perhaps a well structured brainstorm session for ideas on how to tackle the opposition would have been more productive.

David is a fool to himself

Wally Dickson was always late in completing his visit reports. David Wilson could not prepare his weekly report until he had received them. This should have been completed by Friday but it was generally usually the following Tuesday before David could give his report to his boss. Wally's action caused a problem both to David and to David's manager but not to Wally himself.

David often mentioned this to Wally and asked him to get his reports done on time. This he would do for the next week or two before lapsing back into his old, tardy ways.

Eventually, David arranged for Wally to give him a verbal report which David would then write up. This gave David extra work of course, but at least it solved the time problem.

Liz's new tactic

Once a month Liz Cole organised and chaired the management meeting. Marcel Perdue, the Head Chef, was always late in attending, sometimes arriving fifteen minutes after the appointed time. To start with Liz would wait for him before beginning the meeting. This caused the other managers to become annoyed and affected their attitude during the meeting.

Realising that something had to be done, Liz decided to adopt a different tactic. She started the next meeting on time. When Marcel arrived some ten minutes later, he was very surprised to discover the meeting in progress and was obliged to apologise to the group. He managed to arrive on time for future management meetings.

Liz simply removed the benefit from Marcel and thus changed his behaviour.

SUMMARY

Good problem management
- Only attempt to solve those problems that cannot be solved by others.
- Apply the systematic approach.
- Use the technique appropriate to the problem.
- Try to discover the real reasons behind people-related problems.
- Tell people when they are causing you a problem and try to resolve it together.
- Involve other people in finding solutions where you can.
- Evaluate the outcome.

Bad problem management
- Concentrate on action without planning.
- Ignore it, it may go away.
- Believe that you are the only person capable of providing a solution.
- Threaten those who cause you problems.
- Always rely on your experience to solve problems.

DISCUSSION POINTS

1. Think about a major problem that you have recently dealt with. Apply the systematic approach. Would you have reached the same solution?

2. How could David Wilson have changed Wally Dickson's behaviour regarding the visit reports?

3. Brian O'Donnell is the Head of Marketing for a large magazine publishing company. Once a month, he chairs a meeting of his managers.

   The meetings begin with a briefing session where Brian passes down information that he has obtained from the various other meetings he attends during the month. His main objective is to elicit new ideas from his managers. He tries to adopt a participative style but tends not to suffer fools gladly. He is a logical, analytical thinker and these skills are so entrenched that he does not tolerate anything based on 'gut feel' or intuition. As a result he tends to over analyse most of the suggestions put forward during the meeting. This includes pointing out faults and impracticalities.

   As a result, the managers are now reluctant to put forward any new ideas for fear of being made to look foolish in front of their peers. They wait for Brian to produce suggestions.

   Brian believes that the group have become over-dependent on him and resents their reticence. The managers feel that Brian is autocratic and not genuine in inviting their contributions.

   How can Brian rejuvenate his managers and encourage them to participate at the meetings?

   Clue: Whose behaviour needs to be changed and how?

'Give me some good old-fashioned crisis
management at work *any* day.'

9
How to Manage Time

SPOKEN FROM EXPERIENCE

'Time is the friend of one man but the enemy of another' – Chinese Proverb.

'I wasted time, now doth time waste me' (*Richard II*) – Shakespeare.

'There is no correlation between the weight of organisational responsibility you carry and the amount of personal time necessary. The answer is to increase the value of each hour worked, proportionately to your increased responsibility' – Anon.

GETTING THE BALANCE RIGHT

Time is democratic: we all have the same amount. It is what we do with it that really counts. Time ticks by relentlessly. It is very easy to waste but impossible to regain. The only way in which we can 'save' time, is by doing something more quickly or by not doing it at all.

There is 'working' time and 'social' time. If we add to one we automatically take from the other. The art is to maintain a sound balance between the two. As mentioned earlier in this book, the amount of time spent managing should grow with experience, and the amount of time spent doing things should decrease.

As a manager, you need to manage your time carefully, so that you maximise its use and do not encroach upon your 'social' time.

ORGANISING YOUR TIME

Before trying to manage your time effectively, you need to analyse how you spend it at present.

List those activities that you do during the course of a normal week. For example paperwork, telephoning, attending meetings, dealing with people, travelling and so on. Estimate the number of hours you spend on each activity. The total probably exceeds forty hours. Why? In which areas are you spending most of your time? Where should you be spending more? Where are you wasting time? It is hard to admit to wasting time. People usually spend more time than necessary on those tasks they enjoy doing and less on those they dislike.

We operate within three time zones:

- Clock time—the recognised working time, say 9.00am to 5.30pm.

- Goal time—we set ourselves time within which to complete certain tasks. For example we may have to attend a meeting at 3.00pm and set aside two hours in which to prepare for it.

- Hurry up time—this is what we have left of our goal time after interruptions, unplanned jobs etc. You may have to cram two hours' work into one and as a result, rush and make mistakes.

Allocating your time

To ensure that you deal with all of your tasks on time, it is essential to plan how you will use your time effectively.

Your last job each day should be to list everything that you have to do the next day.

- Confirmed appointments, meetings, interviews and so on should be entered in your diary, each with the starting and an estimated finishing time.

- All other tasks, telephone calls, reports and the like, should then be prioritised into:

  (a) must be done tomorrow,

  (b) should be done tomorrow but can be left until next day,

  (c) can be dealt with later.

- The following day, work through this list in order, ticking the tasks as you complete them.

- At the end of the day, revise your list for the day after.

Coping with paperwork

A manager gaining responsibility suffers a geometric increase in paperwork. This is the bane of most managers' lives.

- Action now—this may be something that you must deal with such as a letter of resignation from one of your staff, or something that you can delegate.

- Action later—such as a memo from personnel requesting details of your staff holiday rota. Again decide which you must handle and what can be delegated.

- Information only—direct mail, catalogues, meeting minutes and so on. These can be filed.

Handling interruptions

These are one of the main consumers of a manager's time. If you are engaged in a task and interrupted by a person or by the telephone, by the time you have dealt with it, you have to spend more time collecting your original train of thought. How can you avoid, or at least reduce, such interruptions?

Telephone
- If you have a secretary, ask her to take your calls for a specific period of time.
- Bar your telephone.
- If neither is possible, state firmly that you will call back when it is convenient.

Personal
- Ask your secretary to keep out unwanted visitors.
- Condition your staff not to interrupt you at certain times. Put a 'closed' notice on your desk.
- Make appointments to see people.

HANDING BACK OTHER PEOPLE'S PROBLEMS

Until they have learned otherwise, managers will spend much of their time solving other people's problems, particularly those of their staff.

When one of your staff comes to you with a problem, how often do you say, 'Leave it with me'? This is sometimes known as the 'monkey' syndrome. Each time a person comes to see you with a problem they are said to arrive with a monkey on their back. As soon as you say 'Leave it with me', the monkey jumps from their back onto yours. From then, until you give them a solution, *they* will be managing *you* and your time. If you collect three or four monkeys each day, you will have a menagerie by the end of the week and it will be extremely difficult to do any real work at all.

Apart from giving you extra work, you will not be helping your staff by solving the problems for them. Instead, ask what they have done to solve them, what else they could do and offer suggestions where necessary. This will not only help in their development but, by adopting this approach, they will be less likely to ask you for help until they have exhausted all avenues open to them.

OTHER TIME WASTERS

Problem	Possible solutions
Becoming too involved	Delegate more.
Too much work from above	Learn to say 'no'.
Work piling up	Set priorities and deadlines.
Too much to write	Use the telephone more.
Too much to read	Do you need to read it?
Putting off unpleasant jobs	Set a timetable and do these jobs first.
Disorganised	Work to a system, use your diary.
Firefighting	Distinguish between important and urgent, plan ahead, do one job at a time.
Lack of self-discipline	Set yourself standards, prioritise.
Meetings	See below.

Remember that 20 percent of your time and energy will produce 80 percent of the results (Pareto's Rule).

HOW TO SAVE YOUR TIME BY MANAGING OTHER PEOPLE

Your staff
Delegate as much as possible.
Help them to solve their own problems.
Tell them that you need 'quiet time'.

Your colleagues
Educate them to avoid unnecessary interruptions.
Avoid idle chat.
Deal with them as quickly as possible.

Your manager
Discuss plans and schedules with your boss so that tasks delegated by him to you, fit into your schedule.
Learn to cut discussion short, politely.

MANAGING MEETINGS

The dictionary defines meetings as 'a coming together of a number of persons at a certain time and place, especially for discussion.

Meetings are notorious consumers of people's time, so how can they be used effectively to take up less time?

As a manager, you will be involved in two types of meetings, those that you organise yourself and those that you are asked to attend.

Organising meetings
All meetings should be well planned in order to be effective. Before arranging a meeting, you need to ask yourself the following questions:

Why do I need a meeting?
There must be a definite purpose. Too many meetings take place based on tradition. 'We always have a meeting on Monday morning!'

What do I want to achieve?
Set an objective. Don't try to cover too many topics at one meeting. Three is sufficient, otherwise the meeting will take too long.

Who should I ask to attend?
Only invite those people who really need to be there.

When should I hold it?
Decide on a convenient time and date. Give at least twenty-four hours' notice to the people concerned.

Where should the meeting take place?
The venue should be large enough to accommodate everyone comfortably and be free from interruptions.

Purpose of a meeting
You should only call a meeting in the following circumstances:

- When decisions require judgement rather than just expertise.
- To discuss multi-faceted problems that need different skills.
- When the decision affects all the members.

AGENDA

Purpose: To discuss the maintenance of the new milling machines.

Date: 3rd September 199X

Start Time: 11.30 am

Finish Time: 12.45 pm

Participants:

John Mason (Production Manager) – Chairman
Eric Davies (Chief Production Engineer)
Sarah Dawson (Day Shift Supervisor)
Alan Pearson (Night Shift Supervisor)
Roy Evans (Maintenance Manager)
Mike Simpson (Maintenance Engineer)

Topics:

1 Delivery and installation of new machines	-10 min
2 Training of engineers	- 30 min
3 Maintenance schedules	- 30 min
4 Any other business	- 5 min

If you have anything that you wish to discuss under AOB, please tell the chairman before the meeting.

Figure 7. Example of an agenda.

- When the matter requires group discussion to avoid bias.
- When the information is of value to all the participants.

To make meetings work, there are three things that must happen:

- They should be set up properly.
- There should be a good chairman.
- Those attending should be able to participate effectively.

Preparing agendas

Whenever you arrange a meeting, you should prepare an agenda to be distributed to all participants, at least twenty-four hours before the meeting.

Every agenda should include the following:

- Purpose of the meeting. It is essential that people are made aware of the reason for the meeting and its objective.
- Date.
- Start and finish times. By putting both start and finish times, it will provide a defined amount of time for the meeting. If you begin meetings before a natural break such as lunch or the end of the day, there is a better chance of them finishing on time. It is common knowledge that meetings will expand to fill the time available.
- Venue.
- Participants.
- Topics to be discussed with approximate timings. If any of the members is to give a presentation, that person's name should be included.
- Any other business. This is often a great time waster. To help you to control it, anyone who has anything that they wish to discuss should give you notice of this well before the meeting. It is then for you to decide whether or not it should be included. Too often the items raised only concern one or two people and are better dealt with at another time.

An example of a typical agenda is shown in Figure 7.

Choosing the venue

Wherever you decide to hold the meeting, it is vital that there are no interruptions. How will you arrange adequate seating, lighting and ventilation? On occasion it may be better to have the meeting away from the work place, at an hotel for example.

Psychology plays an important role in a meeting, especially if the subject matter is contentious. Most meetings take place around a rectangular table and the seats at either end are the most powerful. Thus, as the chairman you should take the seat of power. It is a common fact that people seated to your right, will generally be more cooperative. Therefore, if you know that certain people will initially be against your proposal you should arrange for them to sit on our right. Left to themselves, they will sit as far away from you as possible, on the left side of the table.

Figure 8 illustrates the various psychological positions:

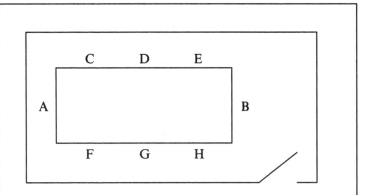

Position A is the most powerful and should be taken by you as the chairman. B is the next most important and should be occupied by your closest ally. Seat those people who you believe have not reached a decision at C, D and E. Participants who are against the proposal are allocated positions F, G and H.

Figure 8. The psychology of seating.

Role of the chairman

The success of a meeting will largely depend upon the effectiveness of the chairman. Ideally, this person should be neutral. However, this is not always practical in a business situation. Therefore, as you have called the meeting, you should take this role.

As chairman, you need to:

- Start by clearly defining the objectives of the meeting.
- Ensure that a conclusion is reached and recorded for each item on the agenda.

- Open the discussion for each topic by setting the scene.
- Invite contributions from each member.
- Keep order when people drift from the point.
- Encourage all points of view.
- Do not dominate the discussion.
- Do not be judgemental.
- Summarise what has been agreed during and at the end of the meeting.
- Agree action plans and further meetings (if necessary).
- Keep an eye on the time and bring the meeting to a close.

Keeping minutes
Where necessary, minutes should be kept during the meeting and distributed to all participants within a couple of days of the meeting.

At the very least, everyone should receive a copy of the action plans, defining who will be doing what.

Attending meetings
When you are asked to attend a meeting, to help you save time you should:

- Check that your attendance is really necessary.
- Obtain a copy of the agenda.
- Carefully plan your participation.
- If only part of the meeting concerns you, arrange to attend only that section.

At the meeting:
- Make your points clearly, succinctly and positively.
- Keep silent if you have nothing to say.
- If unsure, avoid 'I think...'. Instead, question the chairman 'Do you think...?'
- Argue your case firmly, but don't persist with a losing cause.
- Listen and observe.

Well organised and well conducted meetings can be both stimulating and productive.

CASE STUDIES

Arthur's crammed timetable
Arthur Rowe operated to a well planned timetable. Each day began with the meeting with his salesmen. This was followed by an hour-

and-a-half dealing with incoming mail and dictating letters to his secretary. He then spent time observing his salesmen telephoning before returning to his office to write reports, update the graphs and deal with other administration matters.

Afternoons were spent visiting customers, with the exception of Fridays which were devoted to the weekly management meeting.

Unfortunately, this inflexible regime meant that he had no time to deal with his staff. The only time that they could communicate with him was during the morning meeting. Even then their comments and suggestions were given short shrift.

Although you should plan your time, within that plan time needs to be allocated to your staff for delegating, training and so on.

David the firefighter

Because David Wilson was so concerned about the well-being of his staff, his time management was non-existent. Whatever he was asked to do, either by his boss or his team, he found it impossible to say no. As a result, any plans that he may have made soon went out of the window.

The only thing that was sacrosanct was the weekly meeting, although even the time of that had sometimes been changed to accommodate a request from his boss.

Since David spent so much time firefighting, he soon found himself working a fifty hour week and taking work home at weekends. This was having a detrimental affect on his wife and children. Unless he learns to plan his time and stick to the plans, he could well find himself with domestic problems to add to all his others.

Liz keeps control of her time

As a hotel is open for twenty-four hours a day and seven days a week, it would be very easy for Liz Cole to find herself working very long hours.

By delegating as much as possible and only arranging staff meetings when absolutely necessary, she has learned to maximise the time she spends at work. Every morning Liz knows what she has to do during that day. Several of her duties are routine and simple to plan but she always allocates an amount of time to talk to her team and to deal with the unexpected.

The only activity over which Liz does not have control are the managers' meetings that she is obliged to attend. However, she is working on it.

SUMMARY

Good time management

- Plan your time.
- Prioritise your tasks.
- Delegate as much as possible.
- Learn to say 'no'.
- Plan time for your team.
- Be flexible.
- Only hold meetings when necessary.
- Prepare agendas.
- Chair meetings effectively.
- Question the need to attend meetings.

Bad time management

- Being disorganised.
- Becoming too involved, especially in areas that do not concern you.
- Failing to delegate effectively.
- Welcoming interruptions.
- Spending too much time on the tasks that you enjoy.
- Organising and attending too many meetings.
- Poorly conducted meetings.

DISCUSSION POINTS

1. How could you use your work time more effectively?

2. List the meetings that you can arrange and attend during a typical month. Which ones are really necessary?

3. Your manager calls you into his office at 10.00am one Friday and asks you to prepare a report on your suggestions for reducing costs in your department. He needs the information for a meeting at 3.00pm. You estimate that it will take at least three hours to complete this task and it will disrupt your 'end of week' schedule. How will you respond?

10
How to Manage Innovation

SPOKEN FROM EXPERIENCE

'To innovate is not to reform.' – Edmund Burke.

'The most important thing I have learned about management is that the executive must arouse the individual initiative of the men working under him.' – Alfred P Sloan.

'Management of change and innovation is probably the most critical and pervasive task facing business and industry today.' – William T Brady.

LOGICAL VS CREATIVE THINKERS

According to the dictionary, to innovate is 'to make changes, to introduce new things'. It is very much part of the manager's job to introduce 'new things'. However, many people find it very hard to come up with new ideas, particularly to order.

One of the main reasons for this is our conditioning whilst at school. There, we were taught to think logically or, as Edward de Bono puts it, vertically. That is, when faced with a problem we start at the beginning and work through a logical sequence of steps in an attempt to find a solution. In many instances this is quite suitable, but whilst doing so we are unlikely to produce any new ideas or solutions. This traditional approach is too often based upon past experience.

New ideas and solutions are produced through creative or lateral thinking. This is about disregarding the orthodox, being illogical and avoiding the step-by-step approach. The creative thinker will some-times start with a possible solution and work back to discover whether or not it is feasible. The lateral thinker is never convinced that 'it will not work', until it is proven to be so.

The differences
The main differences between the logical thinker and the creative thinker are:

Logical thinker	*Creative thinker*
Chooses	Changes
Looks for what is right	Looks for what is different
Thinks within self-imposed parameters	Discards all parameters
Thinks sequentially	Makes deliberate jumps
Concentrates on the most likely	Explores the least likely
Starts at the beginning	Starts anywhere

One of the main barriers to lateral thinking are the self-imposed parameters. We saddle ourselves with these without exploring whether or not they actually exist.

Remembering this, can you link the nine dots above with four straight lines, without taking your pen or pencil from the paper? See page 144 for the answer.

GENERATING NEW IDEAS

New solutions and ideas often occur when we are doing something quite unconnected with the problem, such as driving the car, walking the dog or watching television.

However, part of your management time should be devoted to innovation. But how? To help you to generate new ideas:

- Explore all possible angles.
- List all approaches without evaluation.
- Switch from problem to problem.
- Allow your mind to wander over alternative and apparently irrelevant ways of looking at the situation.
- Don't spend too much time on a problem if your mind is blank.
- Write down your ideas and thoughts.

Can you solve these problems?
Below is an example of a problem, with both the logical and creative approaches to solving it.

Situation: A singles knock-out tennis tournament has 111 entrants.

Problem: How many matches will have to be played?

Logical approach: Starting with 111, there will be 55 matches in the first round with one player getting a bye. With 56 players remaining there will be 28 matches in the 2nd round, 14 in the 3rd, 7 in the 4th, 3 in the 5th with one bye, 2 semi-finals and the final. A total of 110 matches.

Creative approach: There can only be one eventual winner of the tournament. Therefore there will be 110 losers, one per match.

Apply your creative thinking to the following two problems:

1. *Situation*: An ambulance with an emergency case on board is driving down a narrow country lane. It meets a flock of sheep being driven by a shepherd and his dog, in the same direction as the ambulance.
   Problem: How to get the ambulance past the sheep as quickly and safely as possible.
2. *Situation*: After teeing off, a golfer discovers that his ball has landed inside a paper bag. If he removes the ball from the bag, he will incur a penalty stroke. If he attempt to hit the ball the bag will cause too much resistance for a proper shot.
   Problem: What should the golfer do to avoid a penalty and give himself the chance of hitting a good shot.

See pages 144-145 for possible solutions.

INVOLVING OTHERS

As a manager, you need to encourage your staff to put forward their ideas and suggestions. After all, new ideas are not your sole prerogative and others may have better solutions. This can be achieved by:

- Inviting your staff to tell you about their ideas at any time.
- Listen, without comment, criticism or evaluation.
- Discuss the feasibility of the solution.
- Consider the pros and cons with the person.
- Accept and action appropriate ideas and solutions.

BRAINSTORMING

It is not always possible, or advisable, to spend time alone trying to think of new solutions, especially to those problems which will affect others. In such cases it can be a very useful exercise to gather the group together and run a brainstorming session.

Figure 9. Flipchart from a brainstorm on title for house magazine for Aspley Ltd, a packaging company.

The objective is to generate a large number and variety of solutions to a problem. However, to be successful, there are a number of rules to apply:

- There should be no leader. Thus, as the manager, you must simply become part of the group.

- Define the problem clearly. This ensure that everyone is trying to solve the same problem.

- There should be no pre-announced time limit. This will immediately impose a parameter.

- All ideas and suggestions are written on a flip chart for all to see. Ask one of the group to act as the scribe. The ideas should be scattered on the sheets, if they are listed, they automatically assume a priority. See the sample in Figure 9.

- There must be no criticism, evaluation or judgement at this stage. All suggestions, however silly they may appear, must be written down because they may spark off other ideas.

- When the ideas have dried up evaluate, with the group, those produced into three categories:
  (a) those for immediate use,
  (b) those requiring further investigation,
  (c) those to be discarded.

If any of these rules are broken, the session will not succeed and those involved will be more dubious about future brainstorms.

The main benefits of a well structured brainstorm session are:

- Many new ideas will be generated.
- Every person and suggestion is equally valued.
- Everyone is involved.
- There is more likelihood of commitment for those solutions accepted and acted upon.
- No-one should feel inhibited.
- It should be fun.

The ideal sized group will be between five and fifteen people. This will give everyone an equal chance to take part.

Brainstorming need not be confined to members of your team. It can be a useful exercise to invite people from other departments to attend. People closely involved with the problem may be reluctant to suggest ideas that have not worked in the past, but people who are more remote from the problem will not know that 'it won't work'.

Example

The manager of the despatch department of a company that supplied aquariums directly to customers, was concerned about the high cost of packaging and the increase in breakages reported by customers. He organised a brainstorm to which he invited staff from accounts, sales, production and administration as well as his own department.

The idea which was accepted (to send the products flat-packed) came from someone in accounts.

ACTIONING IDEAS

Coming up with a new idea is only half the solution. The other half is to get it accepted and actioned. Many good ideas die at this point because the manager involved is unable to put them into action.

To be an effective innovator you need to:

- Have a clear view of the results you want to achieve.
- Define clearly the aims and benefits.
- Argue the case persuasively.
- Get support from as many people as possible.
- Have the courage to take calculated risks.
- Be good at getting people to act.
- Have the power to mobilise support and resources.
- Be able to handle interference and opposition.
- Have the force of character to maintain momentum.

CASE STUDIES

Arthur dismisses an idea

Derek Green, one of Arthur Rowe's salesmen, was concerned at how much unproductive time he and his colleagues spent on the telephone. He had an idea how to overcome this. At one of the morning meetings, he decided to put his ideas to the manager.

'Mr Rowe', he began, 'I'm sure you will agree that we spend a great deal of time on the phone, which could be more productively spent in front of customers.'

'Well?' said Arthur, gruffly.

'If we had one or two people who made appointments on our behalf, we could spend more time selling,' Derek explained.

'No, it wouldn't work,' was Arthur's response and that was the end of that. An idea, which could have increased revenue far in excess of the extra cost, was discarded without further consideration. Why? Probably because Arthur had not thought of it first.

David wastes time

David Wilson certainly encouraged his team to be innovative. He began every meeting by asking for any new ideas. Because of David's tendency to explore in great depth every suggestion made, his staff were reluctant to make too many, as they knew only too well how much time would be wasted in discussion.

One problem which David faced was how to simplify visit reports. He asked his team to come up with some ideas for the next meeting. This they duly did: one solution from each person. None was ideal and all were based on past experience. Each was discussed and eventually a compromise was reached and put into action.

Obviously David had never heard of brainstorming.

Liz arranges some brainstorming

Liz Cole was given the task of organising a day's entertainment to thank the hotel's thirty major clients for their custom during the past year.

But what should she organise for these clients? She decided to arrange a brainstorm session to generate some ideas. Representatives from all parts of the hotel were invited to attend. These included kitchen staff, chambermaids and barmen as well as her own team.

Suggestions ranged from a banquet, a day at the races and a river trip, to helicopter flights over London and a car rally. Each idea was evaluated by the group and eventually it was agreed to combine two of the suggestions, one from a waiter and the other from a receptionist. The guests would spend the day playing golf at Wentworth and then return to London by luxury coach for a dinner and dance at the hotel.

As everyone had been involved in the decision, the event proved a great success.

SUMMARY

Good innovation management

- Think creatively.
- Encourage staff to offer new ideas.
- Don't be critical or judgemental.
- Organise brainstorm sessions.
- Be ready to try something different.
- Make every effort to action new ideas.

Bad innovation management
- Always take the logical approach.
- The manager should be the only innovator.
- Take care, not risks.
- Only rely on past experience to solve problems.

DISCUSSION POINTS

1. List three current problems that might be solved by brainstorming.

2. You are given a large, circular cake. How many pieces can you divide it into with four straight cuts?

3. *Situation*: A farmer has a field shaped as below, he also has four sons. Upon his death the field must be divided equally between his sons.

   Problem: How will you divide the land so that each son has one piece of land of equal size?

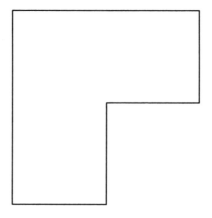

For possible solutions to 2 and 3 above, see page 145.

11
How to Manage Interviews

SPOKEN FROM EXPERIENCE

'Get the facts first, you can distort them later.' – Mark Twain.

'If one tells the truth, one is sure sooner or later to be found out.' – Oscar Wilde.

'An interview is a formal discussion where one person does the talking and the other doesn't listen.' – Anon.

MANAGING DIFFERENT TYPES OF INTERVIEWS

When the word interview is mentioned in a business context it normally conjures up images of recruitment interviews. This chapter is devoted to the other important types of interview in which managers become involved, counselling, correction, grievance and appraisals. All such interviews are conducted between a manager and a member of his or her staff.

An interview is 'A meeting of people, two or more, face to face, to accomplish a certain known purpose'. In reality, an interview should be confined to two persons. Why?—because otherwise it is in danger of becoming a meeting.

Whilst a systematic approach can help to improve skill, too rigid a routine is not recommended. The personalities and circumstances involved will determine how each interview is dealt with.

YOUR FOUR-POINT INTERVIEW PLAN

Whatever the type of interview, it will help you to stick to the following plan:

- Purpose—be sure of your objective. What do you hope to achieve? Most interviews are problem based, ie one of the parties has a problem. Thus the objective should be to find a mutually acceptable solution.

- Prepare—obtain as much information as possible beforehand.

- Conduct
  Allow enough time.
  Ensure privacy.
  Explain the reason for the interview.
  Explain the present situation, clearly and concisely.
  Stimulate the interviewee to respond by use of questions;
    change of tempo and so on.
  Listen—both to what is said and not said.
  Observe the interviewee (body language).
  Check all facts and observations.
  Reach an agreed solution.

- Check results—follow up by another interview or informal chat.
  Check on performance, attitudes, relationships and so on.

PLANNING YOUR INTERVIEW

With the exception of a grievance, the interviews will be instigated by you, the manager. You should, therefore, ensure that you have prepared properly and sufficiently and obtained as much background information as posible.

Arranging the seating

How the interviewer and interviewee are seated will have a strong influence on the progress and outcome of the interview.

(a)

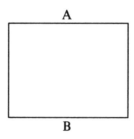

When two people sit on opposite sides of a desk or table, it is known as the competitive position. The desk forms a physical barrier with the people facing each other eyeball to eyeball. This is how one would sit when playing chess or some other competitive activity. It is not conducive for open discussion.

(b)

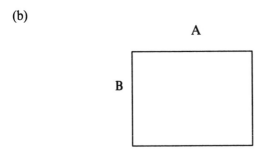

The corner position removes the barrier whilst enabling the people to sit so as not to infringe each other's 'comfort zone'. They are not obliged to constantly look at one another and this removes much of the pressure.

(c)

Sitting side by side is the cooperative position. It would be used when training someone on a one-to-one basis, as it enables the learner to see exactly what the trainer is doing and vice versa.

(d)

With the open position there is no desk or table, just two chairs. These are positioned at an angle to each other to remove the necessity for the people to look at one another. It is designed to promote open, honest discussion and is excellent for observing body language.

HANDLING COUNSELLING INTERVIEWS

Counselling is normally undertaken by well trained and highly skilled counsellors. However, the term may also be applied to an interview where a manager is trying to discover a problem 'owned' by an employee and find a solution for it. Many of the techniques discussed here apply to all types of interviews.

You would arrange a counselling interview when you have observed a change in the behaviour of one of your staff which has not given cause for correction. The purpose is to discover the cause and to reach a mutually acceptable solution. It is not to give advice or offer solutions.

Many managers refrain from counselling because they do not know how to start the interview. Don't beat about the bush. It is easier to come straight out with your reason for the interview, eg 'I've noticed that you seem rather lethargic lately. It is not like you and it concerns me. What has happened to cause this?' Always ask a direct question and wait for a naswer. There may be a few moments of silence but don't panic, give the person time to think and supply an answer. Do not say 'Do you have a problem?' as you may well get a defensive 'No' as an answer.

The person that you are interviewing will usually give you an initial reason for their behaviour. It may be a simple, surface reason which is easy for them to talk about. This is known as the presenting problem. If you attempt to solve it, you will only be part way to a complete solution.

Inevitably there will be a deeper seated problem, which your interviewee will be reluctant initially to discuss. This is the core problem. It is vital to unearth this for only by solving the core problem will the behaviour of the person change for the better.

The way to reach this core problem is by asking elaboration questions and then waiting patiently for an answer. Time can be a valuable clue. If you noticed a change in the person's behaviour three months ago, ask them if anything happened at that time. The answer can often be most revealing.

Counselling can be a very delicate operation. Remember that you are asking a member of your staff to reveal personal information. For counselling to be successful they must trust and respect you and know that whatever they say will be treated in the strictest confidence.

Never criticise, judge or take sides. As soon as you do, you might as well bring the interview to a close there and then. Ask questions, listen carefully to the answers and reflect back.

Stimulating solutions

Once you have discovered the core problem, you need to get the person to solve it for themselves with your help. Ask them how they think they could solve it, and to explain the consequences of their solutions.

Give the employee relevant information but never offer your own solution. The interviewee may accept it on the surface, but will not act upon it with any conviction. If you are asked for a solution, use the 'third party reference', eg 'Mary Thompson in Personnel had a similar problem and what she did was to...'.

Checking the results

Once an acceptable solution has been reached, agree an action plan and offer to discuss the outcome after a defined period of time. It may be that you know the suggested solution will not work, but providing it will not do any damage, allow your employee to find that out for themselves.

Counselling requires practice and is not always successful. It may well take two or more interviews before a solution is reached but do not lose heart.

Example of a counselling interview

Martin Dobson was the manager of the data processing department of a large financial institution. He had noticed that one of his staff, Don Huntley, had become rather introverted and no longer went to lunch with his colleagues, preferring to eat a sandwich at his work station. This concerned Martin, for Don was normally a very gregarious person. He decided to counsel Don to find out the reason for this change.

Martin began by saying. 'Many thanks for coming to see me Don. I've noticed that you seem to spend more time by yourself lately. This concerns me as it isn't like you, you used to be the life and soul of the office. Is there any reason for this?'

'No, not really,' Don replied after a few moments. Martin said nothing. 'I'm just a bit fed up,' Don continued.

'I see,' said Martin. 'It was about three months ago that I noticed you spending more time alone. Did anything happen at that time?'

'Just a personal matter,' replied Don after a further period of silence.

'A personal matter,' Martin reflected.

'Yes.'

'Ah ha.'

Martin then remained quiet until Don eventually broke the silence.

'I'd been going out with this girl for about two years, everything was going well and we became engaged. Then, three months ago, she suddenly broke it off with no explanation. I don't know why.'

'You felt upset when she ended your engagement,' Martin said without emotion.

'I was shattered,' Don replied bitterly. 'She gave me no reason, just gave me back the ring and that was that.'

'How did you feel about yourself when this happened?' Martin asked.

'Rejected and degraded,' Don said. 'How can you face your mates when they know you've been given the big E?'

'Did you tell your friends that your relationship with this girl had ended?' asked Martin.

'I had to tell my close friends as we all used to go out as a group,' said Don.

'What was their reaction?'

'Most were quite sympathetic and said that I was better off without her.'

'They felt sorry for you. Do you still go out with these friends?'

'Sometimes with the lads for a drink.'

'Have you told any of your work colleagues about this?'

'No, they'd only have a laugh.'

'You believe that they might act differently from your other friends?'

'I don't know really.'

'They are as worried about you as I am. So what can we do to change the situation?'

'I suppose I could tell them and try to be a bit more cheerful.'

'How easy do you think that will be?'

'It'll be difficult trying to be cheerful as I still feel that it was my fault and there must be something wrong with me.'

'How can you overcome that feeling?'

'I don't know, what do you suggest?'

'About two years ago, a similar thing happened to a friend on mine and he felt very depressed for months. Then he joined a club for single and divorced professional people and now he enjoys a very active social life. It completely changed his outlook on life.'

'That's an idea. I'll give it a try.'

'OK Don, thank you for being so open with me and I can asssure you that what you have said remains strictly between us. Let's have another chat in a couple of months and see how things are going.'

When Don said that he was fed up, Martin decided not to pursue that line and moved straight to the 'time' question. This brought the desired response from Don and the core problem was revealed. Being a difficult personal problem Martin resorted to the 'third party reference' in answer to Don's request for help.

HANDLING CORRECTION INTERVIEWS

These are more often referred to as disciplinary interviews. However, your objective should be to discover the reason for the employee's misdemeanour and to correct the behaviour leading to it. Thus correction is a more appropriate term.

Nobody misbehaves or makes errors simply for the sake of it; there is always a good reason. It is very easy to reprimand a member of your staff if they step out of line. What will be the effect? How do *you* feel when you are on the receiving end of such a reprimand? Angry, afraid, apathetic? It will be an emotional feeling coupled with negative thoughts about the person disciplining you. You may well change your behaviour, but it will be done grudgingly and it will not take much for you to slip back into your old ways. This is because the real reason for your behaviour remains active.

A correction interview needs to be conducted very like a counselling interview. Explain the reason for the interview and the consequences of the matter under discussion. Try and discover the core reason and ask the employee to suggest ways to alter his or her behaviour.

At the end of a correction interview there should be two winners, you and your employee.

Example of a correction interview

Eileen Murray was the supervisor of the credit control department of a contract catering company. It had recently come to her notice that one of her most valued staff, Brian Stoke, had been making uncharacteristic mistakes in his figure work. Several errors had slipped through the system and brought angry complaints from customers.

Eileen knew that anyone can make an error, but Brian was now making too many to be acceptable. It was time to take action. Eileen was tempted to call Brian into her office, give him a strong reprimand and tell him to be more careful in the future. However, she realised that there was more to it than simple carelessness.

She gathered together examples of the mistakes and arranged an appointment to see Brian in her office.

'As you know Brian', Eileen began 'I've always been very pleased with the high degree of accuracy you have shown in your work. So I am surprised and disappointed to see an increasing number of errors creeping in lately. Is there any reason for this?'

'No,' Brian replied, petulantly. 'Anyone can make mistakes.'

'That's true,' said Eileen, 'but it's unlike you to make so many. There have been fourteen critical errors during the last three weeks.'

'Checking up on me are you?' Brian retorted.

'Not checking up, just making sure of my facts as it is so unlike you.' Eileen remained calm. 'You are a very important member of our team, so I'm sure you are aware of the consequences of these mistakes.'

'So, what's happened?' Brian asked.

'Well, six our customers have expressed their annoyance and unfortunately two of them phoned our MD direct, so naturally he wants to know what is going on,' Eileen explained. 'So I am hoping that you can tell me why there has been this decrease in your accuracy?'

Brian thought for a few moments and Eileen remained silent. 'I suppose I'm bored,' Brian said finally.

'Bored,' Eileen confirmed.

'Yes, I've been doing the same job for two years now and I don't seem to be getting anywhere,' said Brian.

'So you are feeling frustrated,' reflected Eileen.

'Yes I am,' said Brian. 'I had hoped that I would be doing something more interesting by now. I'll never get promoted at this rate.'

'You feel that you need work that will stretch and develop you,' Eileen said.

'I want to feel that I am being used to my potential,' Brian replied.

'Right, how can we help you to achieve this?'

'You could delegate some of your work to me.'

'If I did that, would you still be able to handle your present tasks?'

'No problem. I have to make the work last to fill the time as it is.'

'So, if I delegate work to you and train you to do it, you will feel much happier.'

'I certainly will.'

'Good. We'll meet again at 10.00 am on Thursday and that will give me time to sort out some suitable tasks for you. I'm so glad that we have been able to solve this matter to our mutual benefit.'

It could be said that it was Eileen's fault that Brian was forced to make mistakes in his work to get her attention and provide an opportunity to explain his needs.

HANDLING GRIEVANCE INTERVIEWS

A grievance is a real or imagined cause for complaint by one or more people against others. Many such complaints in industry are by groups of people against the company or organisation they work for. These grievances are normally handled by the trade union, staff council or similar body.

The grievances that face an individual manager will be between members of his or her staff. One of your team may approach you with a complaint against a colleage and expect you to sort it out there and then. A natural reaction would be to reprimand the person against whom the complaint has been made.

The correct way to handle such grievances is firstly to interview the complainant. Handle it as you would a counselling session. Obtain as much information as possible about the incident leading to the dispute. If necessary you can follow up with a similar interview with the person complained about.

During these interviews, you may uncover a deep seated cause 'owned' by one of the people concerned. If this is the case, encourage the person to seek their own solutions, as in counselling.

If no such problem is revealed, call the people together; with you acting as counsellor, encourage them to reach an acceptable solution by discussion.

Example of a grievance interview

Ray Macpherson was sitting in his office one morning, when Sally Robinson, one of his staff, burst through the door.

'That's it, I've had enough,' she cried. 'You must do something about Bob. He sits there puffing away on his revolting pipe, blowing smoke all over me and I can't take any more.'

Ray invited Sally to take a seat. After she had calmed down, he began to ask her to explain the situation. She said the Bob's smoking habit had been annoying her for the past month. It also transpired that it was at about that time that Sally had begun revising for her exams. She studied late into the night, was tired when she came to work and this had made her very irritable. The exams were to take place the following week. When Ray asked what could be done to ease the problem, Sally suggested that she took some leave until after the exams. Ray agreed and the matter was solved. It had not been necessary to talk to Bob although, having heard about the complaint, he confined his smoking to the coffee breaks in future.

HANDLING APPRAISAL INTERVIEWS

An **appraisal** is a formal review of an employee's performance with his or her immediate manager and an opportunity to set future targets.

There are all kinds of appraisal systems and many companies operate them differently. However, the core of any appraisal should be an interview. Even if your company does not have an official appraisal scheme, there is no reason why you should not conduct appraisal interviews with your staff.

The interview will be based upon the key tasks as set out in the job descriptions. Don't treat it as a formal opportunity to criticise each member of your staff. Make it a positive and motivating experience.

Format for appraisal interviews

- Ask your employee how they believe they have performed, during the period under review, against each key task.
- Listen without criticism or judgement.
- If the performance is below the accepted standard, ask the employee why this has happened and what they could do to improve.
- Praise good performances.
- Document comments on performance.
- Agree new targets and key tasks and put them in writing with a copy for the employee.

If your staff trust and respect you, they will be open and honest about their own performances.

By involving your team in the setting of their targets, you will gain their commitment to achieve them. If their expectations fall below your requirements, you will need to use your negotiation skills. If you impose targets, you may get the person's agreement but not their commitment. Should they fail to achieve these targets, they will remind you that they were your targets not theirs.

Ideally, you need to undertake appraisal interviews every six months.

CASE STUDIES

Arthur: 'No excuses!'
As you would expect, Arthur Rowe's approach to appraisals, was somewhat authoritarian.

'Right Davis, come in and sit down, it's time for the annual appraisal,' was Mr Rowe's introduction. 'I've written my comments about your performance, so just read it through and sign it.'

Gareth Davis began to read. 'I don't really agree that my paperwork is not up to scratch,' he protested.

'Those are my views,' replied Arthur. 'You don't put enough details on your visit reports. I've told you about this before.'

Gareth read on. 'But I have tried to reach the new accounts target that you set last year. It's not my fault that the competition have a better system,' he said.

'Listen young man, I don't want excuses. These are the facts, so just sign,' retorted Arthur.

Reluctantly Gareth signed the report.

'Right, I want you to increase your revenue by 15 percent during the next year,' demanded Arthur.

Gareth left the office realising there was no room for discussion.

David skates over things

David Wilson took the opposite view when it came to appraising his staff's performance.

'Hello Deirdre, sit down, it's appraisal time once again,' David began. 'So how have things been going?'

'Fine,' replied Deirdre. 'We could do with more resources, that would help.'

'Yes, I agree,' said David. 'Anything else?'

'Not really, but we do seem to waste a lot of time with all the staff meetings,' she commented.

'Yes, I really must try and do something about that,' David responded. 'No other problems?'

'Plenty of problems, but nothing that can't be sorted out.'

'Good. Well if there's anything I can do to help, just let me know.'

'I will.'

'So, I think if we carry on much the same for next year, we'll be all right. Thanks for all your efforts.'

The appraisal was over.

Liz involves the appraisee

Liz Cole arranged the six monthly appraisal interview with Bill Frobisher, the Head Porter.

'Good morning Bill, please take a seat,' Liz began.

'As you know, the purpose of this meeting is to review your performance over the past six months. Overall, I'm very pleased with what you have been doing, but let's look at each of the key tasks and perhaps you will give me your comments.'

'OK, that sounds fine to me,' said Bill.

'The first key task was to ensure that all the conference rooms were set out as required by our clients so that they could begin on time,' Liz said.

'We've been able to achieve that most of the time,' Bill answered. 'The only problems are when the clients change their minds at the last moment and we have to go looking for extra flip charts or projectors. Sometimes we have to hire equipment and this adds to our costs.'

'That's a good point,' Liz replied. 'How do you think we can overcome it?'

'Perhaps we need to take stock of what we have and buy extra items if necessary,' suggested Bill.

'In that case, can we make one of our key tasks to carry out a complete inventory of our conference equipment and make suggestions as to what we need both to replace and increase?' Liz asked.

'Yes, that's fine with me. When do you want it by?'

'How long will it take you?'

'I could do it by the end of the month.'

'Fine, so you'll let me have the list by, say, the 6th of June.'

The rest of the inteview followed much the same pattern and ended with Liz and Bill signing the comments on past performance and Bill having new targets and key tasks for the next six months.

SUMMARY

Good interviewing
- Prepare by obtaining as much information as possible before the interview.
- Ensure privacy.
- Emphasise confidentiality.
- Ask appropriate questions.
- Listen carefully.
- Observe the interviewee's body language.
- Use counselling techniques to discover the core problem.
- Encourage the interviewees to reach their own solution.

Bad interviewing
- Being unprepared.
- Doing most of the talking and failing to listen.
- Judging and criticising.

- Attempting to solve the presenting problem.
- Offering advice.
- Suggesting solutions.

DISCUSSION POINTS

1. Which seating layout would you suggest as being most appropriate to each type of interview?

2. Do you and each member of your team have key tasks? If so, are they appropriate? If not, prepare three or four for each of your staff, with their cooperation.

3. Remembering that your interviewee could be in a highly emotional state, how would you react if the interviewee

   (a) bursts into tears?

   (b) verbally abuses you?

   (c) loudly criticises his or her colleagues?

'Hey man, leave out all this heavy authority-figure stuff!'

12
How to Manage Change

SPOKEN FROM EXPERIENCE

'People have first to decide that they want to change, then they must be encouraged not to be afraid of change and finally they must be able to see where change is leading them.' – Sir John Harvey-Jones.

'Whilst people do not mind change, they do mind being changed.' – D L Foster.

UNDERSTANDING THE CAUSES OF CHANGE

Changes to an organisation are caused by both internal and external factors. Many of these changes are unpredictable and whatever the causes or circumstances, invariably involve people. The way in which people react to change will depend on how the change is presented to them and how they perceive it will affect them.

The causes of change can be divided into two types. Those over which you as a manager have no influence and those over which you do.

In the first group are changes which will affect the whole company, such as relocation or a change in company policy. These are often due to external factors such as the economy, the environment or the law.

Changes which you can influence are normally those which will mainly affect only you and your staff. Perhaps they have been suggested by you and/or your staff, for example, new work methods, delegation and new objectives.

UNDERSTANDING RESISTANCE TO CHANGE

People seldom accept change without complaint or comments, even when it is beneficial. Resistance is natural and before you can overcome it, you need to consider the reasons behind it.

- Habit—people are comfortable working in familar conditions. They become a habit and people do not like to change established habits.

- Conformity—most people like to conform to the accepted ways of working and behaving. Anything which threatens to disrupt this environment will be viewed with suspicion.

- Misunderstanding—people may not understand what the change will mean, and believe that they will lose out as a result. This is usually due to poor communication.

- Threat to their interests—people rarely believe that any changes made by their company will be of benefit to them individually. They will immediately look for negatives not positives.

- Rumours—changes are often preceded by a myriad of rumours perpetrated by those who have only half the story. Such rumours are normally full of gloom and doom.

- Lack of involvement—too often changes are thrust upon people without giving them a chance to question or discuss the implications. Of course it is not always either possible or practical to involve everyone in company-driven changes.

Example of a badly-managed change
The following example illustrates the results of not involving the people to be affected by a change and of poor communication.

Ian Forsyth was the director of a large company involved in making and distributing agricultural chemicals and feedstuffs. In addition to his seat on the board, Ian managed one of the company's main subsidiaries.

One day while Ian was at his golf club, he fell into conversation with a new member who, it transpired, was the mangaging director of a sales training consultancy. He told Ian about a system his compnay had developed to increase the sales performance of firms such as Ian's.

Ian became very interested. After several visits from the consultants, he agreed to putting the new system in the sales department of the subsidiary. As time passed Ian's enthusiasm increased and he was very impressed by the results. He persuaded the main board to adopt the sytem throughout the company. This was agreed, but by no means unanimously.

The company had its own very active and successful sales and managment training department. However, neither they nor the sales force were consulted, which caused immediate resentment among those people concerned. A series of one-day training sessions was set up for all sales managers, sales people and trainers. The last group were included as they would be expected to continue the training after the consultants had left.

It soon became clear that the only differences between this 'new system' and normal good sales practices, were the jargon and paperwork. This only served to add to the resistance.

Once the initial training had been completed, the system was put into operation. Although there was nothing intrinsically wrong with it, because the system had been imposed upon the sales force they only paid it lip service, with the exception of two sales teams who tried to make it work. This was despite the efforts of Ian Forsyth and the consultants.

Within six months the whole idea had been discarded. It was estimated that this débâcle had cost the company some £200,000 in fees to the consultants and printing costs.

If only they had consulted those who were to be involved before introducing the system, it could have been successful and at far less cost. The company's own training department could have been used instead of bringing in expensive, outside consultants.

HOW TO OVERCOME RESISTANCE

Although people will show an initial resistance to changes, this is better than apathy. It is easier to change the former than the latter.

How can you help overcome any resistance to change among your staff? Practise the following as appropriate:

- Preparation—where change has come about as a result of a shift in company policy, such as the introduction of flexi-time, you need to discuss the implications and benefits with your staff before the change takes place. Although it is not possible for your staff to be consulted about the change, they will be ready for it when it happens.

- Information—provide your staff with as much information about the impending change as you can. Tell them the reasons for the change, the benefits, the expected results and so on. This will help to reduce the impact of any rumours.

- Involvement—when practical, involve your staff with the change. If, for example, you are to lose one of your staff, discuss with the team how they will cope with this reduction in their number. Involvement will aid commitment.

- Communication—make sure all the facts are clearly communicated to your staff, with an adequate opportunity for questions and clarifications. This will help to prevent misunderstanding.

- Awareness—make sure that you are aware of any impending changes, preferably before your staff do.

CASE STUDIES

Arthur's fait accompli

Arthur Rowe's sales team were paid their commission in two instalments, 50 percent on order and the balance when the customer had paid. In order to improve cash flow, the board made a decision to change this system and only pay commission once the customer had settled the account. As some customers took as much as ninety days' credit, this meant that the sales staff would have to wait that long before receiving their money.

Arthur broke the news at one of his morning meetings.

'As from the beginning of next month, your commission will only be paid when the customer pays,' were his exact words.

No attempt was made to explain the reasons or allow any discussion. It was present as a *fait accompli*. The result was, that apart from being further demotivated, the salesmen spent much of their time chasing the accounts and credit control departments, causing considerable annoyance. In addition they were reluctant to accept orders from customers taking more than thirty days credit.

David hears a rumour

'I understand that we are going to move to a new office next month', said Tony Rawlins at one of the social service departments many meetings.

'Are we?' exclaimed David Wilson. 'I didn't know about it.'

'Yes, it's all round the Town Hall,' Tony continued.

'Well, I suppose we had better get ourselves prepared,' said David. 'We need to get our files packed and so on.'

'Hang on a minute,' Deirdre interjected, 'don't you think we ought to find out more about it first? Like when and where we are going.'

'Good idea,' said David. 'Perhaps you can gather the facts and we can discuss it at our next meeting.'

As it happened the move was only a rumour resulting from a meeting of the Ways and Means Committee which had discussed possible relocations sometime in the future.

Liz prepares for change

The Head Porter at Liz Cole's hotel was to retire in three months. Liz had already earmarked his successor from among the staff. When Liz mentioned this to her manager, he told her that the directors wished to promote someone from another hotel in the group.

Although this annoyed her, Liz was philosophical about it. She found out as much as she could about the new man and even visited him at his present post.

She arranged a meeting with the porters and explained the situation to them, painting a true and positive picture of their prospective boss. She asked them for their help and suggestions to enable him to settle quickly into his new role.

By the time the new man arrived his staff were well prepared for him. Any initial resistance that they may have had about him was dissipated.

SUMMARY

Good management of change
- Communicate the change clearly.
- Prepare your staff for the change.
- Give your staff as much information as possible.
- Involve your staff where appropriate.
- Quash rumours as quickly as possible.
- Sell the benefits of the change.
- Recognise resistance and fears.
- Be positive about the change.

Bad management of change
- Thrust changes upon your staff.
- Tell your staff that they must accept the change, regardless of the implications.
- Allow no questions or discussions.
- Be unaware of the facts of the change.
- Fail to understand the reasons for the change.

DISCUSSION POINTS

1. How do you think Arthur Rowe should have dealt with the directive from his board about the changes in the payment of commission?

2. How could David Wilson have dealt with Tony Rawlins' comment about moving offices?

3. What may be the positive results of:

   (a) one of your staff being made redundant to save costs?
   (b) relocation to premises twenty miles from your present site?
   (c) the introduction of flexi-time?

'The technology works fine, but it's the human factor
I'm worried about...'

13
How to Manage Stress at Work

SPOKEN FROM EXPERIENCE

'One of the main reasons why people are stressed at work is their boss and the way they are managed.' – Prof. Cary Cooper.

'Britain leads the world in expensive, stress-induced disease.' – Dr Vernon Coleman.

'There is one way for an executive to manage stress. He must stop taking for granted success at home, and begin giving as much priority in terms of time and energy to achieving success there as he does to his job.' – Dr James Gallagher.

If you take a wooden ruler and exert increasing pressure to either end, eventually the material will exceed its stress point and the ruler will break. The same thing can, and does happen to people. Most of us expect, and indeed thrive, on a certain amount of pressure at work. However, when this pressure becomes too great we become stressed, sometimes with devastating results. Different people have different breaking points.

In his book *Stress Management Techniques*, Dr Vernon Coleman states that in the UK stress costs companies £1,000 per employee, per year. Thus a work force of 1,000 will cost £1,000,000 per year. These are expenses that can be dramatically reduced by good management.

UNDERSTANDING THE CAUSES OF STRESS

Contrary to popular belief, the most common causes of stress have their origins outside the workplace. A few years ago a list of activities which can cause stress was compiled by psychologists. It is based on a scale of 0–100. The higher the value, the greater the stress.

Both positive and negative events can cause stress. It is interesting to note that of the thirty-four activities listed over, only seven are directly work related and the highest two will have a direct effect on your domestic life.

The main causes of stress

Activity	Value	Activity	Value
Death of spouse	100	Foreclosure of loan or mortgage	30
Divorce	73		
Legal separation from spouse	65	Change in responsibilities at work	29
Jail sentence	63		
Death of close relative	63	Son or daughter leaving home	29
Personal injury or illness	53		
Getting married	50	Difficulties with spouse's relatives	29
Losing job	47		
Reconciliation with spouse	45	Outstanding personal achievement	28
Retirement	45		
Change in health of close relative	44	Children starting or finishing school	26
Pregnancy	40	Change in living conditions	25
Sexual problems	39	Revision of personal habits	24
New addition to close family	39	Poor relations with work superior	23
Business readjustment	39		
Change in financial state	38	Change in work hours or conditions	20
Death of a close friend	37		
Change of type of work	36	Change of residence	20
Change in number of arguments with spouse	35	Mortgage less than £40,000	17
		Holidays	12
Mortgage above £40,000	31	Christmas	11

By referring to the list, you can estimate how much stress you are suffering from at any one time. Psychologists regard 300 points as being the breaking point for the average person. Eighty percent of people with scores of over 300 and 53 percent with scores between 150 and 300 are likely to suffer some form of stress-related illness.

Stressful occupations
Similarly, some occupations are more likely to induce stress than others. (0-10 scale; high number = high stress).

8.3 Miner
7.7 Police
7.5 Civil airline pilot/prison officer/ journalist
7.3 Dentist
7.2 Actor
6.8 Doctor
6.5 Nurse/midwife
6.3 Fireman/musician
6.2 Teacher
5.8 Manager (commerce)/ marketing/professional sport
5.5 Selling
5.4 Bus driver

5.0 Publishing
4.8 Farmer/diplomat
4.7 Armed forces
4.4 Civil servant
4.3 Accountant/engineer/estate agent/secretary/receptionist, local government officer
4.0 Architect/optician/planner/ postman
3.7 Banking/computing/linguist
3.5 Vicar
2.8 Museum curator
2.0 Librarian

Although management as a profession only has a stress rating of 5.8, some managers seem to spend their time trying to push it as far up the scale as possible. Do you feel that you are in a stressful job? The above list may give you some ideas for a change of occupation.

People who experience domestic pressures often immerse themselves in their work in an attempt to forget these problems. However, the problems are still there when they return home, so they will work longer hours in order to delay having to go home. These increased absences result in still more stress on the domestic front. It is a vicious circle.

There are other happenings at work which, while not appearing to be stressful in themselves, may well contribute to increased and needless pressure on the individual:

Other stressful factors

- Too much work—giving few opportunities to plan or prioritise.

- Too little work—boredom and a sense of being under-valued and ignored.

- Isolation—most people need human contact and those who work alone can be stressed by a lack of communication.

- Routine work—not being stretched or challenged.

- Poor supervision—unable to become involved or use creative abilities.

- No clear promotional structure—frustration.

- Environment—working in cramped conditions, seating arrangements, open plan office, too much noise.

Example of stress management at work

Due to expansion, the head office of a large retail chain moved to larger premises. In order to maximise the space available, most departments were installed in open plan offices.

A few weeks later, Gillian Thomas, who managed the customer relations department, noticed that several of her staff were showing signs of stress. This manifested itself in arguments between the members of the team, increased absenteeism, less communication and people unwilling to work overtime.

Gillian decided to speak to Eileen, her most senior member of staff.
'It's these new offices,' said Eileen. 'They're just not right for us.'
'I see,' said Gillian. 'How do you mean, not right?'

'Well to start with there's too much noise from the rest of the office. We can't hear ourselves properly on the telephone,' Eileen explained.

'Is there anything else?'

'Yes, the position of the desks. Everytime I look up, I look straight at Jean's face or the top of her head. I've nothing against her but she's just too close and I feel pressured. I know several of the other girls feel the same.'

Gillian knew that there was little she could do about the noise. She asked Eileen to get together with the rest of the team and design a plan for repositioning the desks to help to relieve the pressure. This was a comparatively simple solution which reduced tension in the department.

Our need for personal space

Personal space is very important to us. We all have zones into which we only invite certain people. Although the sizes of these zones will depend upon a person's culture, in the UK they are approximately:

- Intimate zone—up to 18 inches—into which we only allow our very closest friends and relatives.
- Personal zone—18 inches to 3 feet—for other friends, relatives and close acquaintances.
- Social zone—3 to 12 feet—most acquaintances, business colleagues and people we have only recently met.
- Public zone—over 12 feet—everyone else.

When people invade these zones without permission we can feel pressurised, even stressed. We try to overcome this by pretending that they are not there. That is why when in a crowded lift, people either look at the floor or the indicator board.

Take a look at the space within your department. Is it planned to minimise the risk of stress?

OBSERVING THE SYMPTOMS OF STRESS

The symptoms differ according to the physical and psychological make-up of the individual and the cause of the stress.

Typical physical symptoms are: anxiety, headaches, muscular pains in chest and back, palpitations, breathing difficulties, disturbances of the bowel, fainting, and tiredness.

As a manager, you may not be able to detect any of these in your staff. However, they are definite signs that may indicate that someone, including yourself, is under too much pressure and heading towards stress. The following are typical stress activities:

Typical stress activities

- Over reaction—to requests, comments, suggestions.

- Under reaction—lack of response to requests and so on.

- Procrastination—reluctance to make decisions.

- More activity than productivity.

- Over tenacity—refusing help.

- Welcoming interruptions.

- Escapism—untypical increased humour when faced with problems or difficulties.

- Perfectionism—too much time spent on detail.

- Impulsive activity—jumping from task to task.

- Dealing with 'important' rather than 'urgent' tasks.

- Over involvement.

- Regular overtime.

- 'Having a finger in every pie'.

- Increased lateness and/or absenteeism.

Look for any of the above signs in yourself, your staff and your superiors.

Example of personal stress

Alex was a senior laboratory technician with a pharmaceutical company and was well regarded by his superiors. His manager noticed that Alex was becoming increasingly tetchy with his colleagues and when asked about the progress he was making with his current project, refused to offer any conclusions.

Realising that all was not well, his manager tried to talk to Alex and discover the reason for his changed behaviour. At first Alex would only say that it was the complexity of his work. Eventually, however, he revealed to his manager that his son had recently been involved in a motor cycle accident and was in intensive care. The manager gave Alex compassionate leave in order to help him to deal with his domestic problem and so relieve him of the added pressures of work.

MANAGING STRESS AT WORK

As far as stress is concerned, prevention is better than cure. There is nothing that you can do to prevent the domestic causes of stress among your staff but there is much that you can do to prevent stress at work. As Professor Cooper says in the quotation at the beginning of this chapter, managers are largely responsible for stress at work. This is mainly due to poor management techniques.

How can you reduce the pressure on your staff? Below is a list of actions that you might take. Indicate those which you believe would be most practical by giving ten points to the most, nine points to the next and so on.

Activity	Points
1. Listen to your staff and give them the opportunity to express their views.	_____
2. Clarify the criteria for career advancement.	_____
3. Make clear what standards are acceptable to you.	_____
4. Encourage staff to analyse their own behaviour, for stress.	_____
5. Involve staff in decision-making.	_____
6. Give praise as and when due.	_____
7. Avoid excessive criticism.	_____
8. Protect staff against excessive workloads.	_____
9. Give staff the opportunity to discuss their problems with you.	_____
10. Encourage staff to pursue out-of-work activities.	_____

You can help to reduce the likelihood of stress at work in both yourself and your staff by practising the following:

- Establish priorities—decide the importance of the main tasks you need to perform during the working day. Remember some of your private life needs to be fitted into the scheme.

- Manage your time—allocate to the less important tasks only the time they need, no more.

- Delegate—this give you more time for the priorities.

- Communicate—avoid isolation, get out of your office and talk to people.

As we have seen, much stress is domestic in its origin. There are things that you can do and encourage your staff to do to help prevent stress:

- Relax—do not take work home. If you do then you need to look at your priorities, time management and delegation.

- Exercise—take regular physical exercise, but never overdo it as this can cause further physical problems. The medical profession have proven that a brisk walk is more beneficial than jogging.

- Hobbies—undertake one or more absorbing hobbies, these will help to relax the mind.

- Diet—eat sensibly to prevent vitamin and mineral deficiencies and reduce calorie intake, unless you are able to burn them off with physical exercise.

- Devote more time to resolving family problems—after all this is where most of the stress comes from.

RELAXATION TECHNIQUES

Do you find it difficult to relax? There are a number of simple exercises than can help. It is a matter of alternately tensing and relaxing each group of muscles. For example, relaxation of the arms:

- Sit back in your chair as comfortably as possible, breathe in and out normally, close your eyes and relax completely.
- Keep relaxed but clench your right fist.
- Make the muscles of your lower arm and hand even tighter.
- Monitor the feelings of tension.
- Now relax. Let all the tension go.
- Allow the muscles of your lower arm and hand to become completely limp and loose.
- Notice the contrast in feelings.
- Repeat the above three times.
- Do the same with your left hand and lower arm.
- Keeping your right hand and lower arm as relaxed as possible, bring your right elbow into the back of the chair and press downwards contracting the bicep muscles.
- Monitor the feeling.
- Observe the difference.
- Repeat three times.
- Do the same with your left arm.

These, and similar exercises can be carried out at work, at home and whilst travelling—be careful if you are driving.

If you want to practise more advanced relaxation techniques such as yoga or self-hypnosis, seek expert advice.

CASE STUDIES

Arthur: 'Stress is weakness'

Although he may not have realised it, Arthur Rowe's morning meetings put extra pressure onto his sales team. So did his habit of checking them when using the telephone and his closed door policy, which prevented them from asking questions or making suggestions.

Managers such as Arthur still regard stress as a sign of weakness and failure. Rather than admit that they were under strain his salesmen would leave and seek employment with a manager with a more acceptable management style.

David multiplies the stress

Much of the work done by David Wilson's team was of a highly emotional nature and produced its own stress. In order to protect his staff from additional pressures, David took on most of the extra tasks himself. However this, together with his policy of encouraging open discussion of all topics, had the opposite effect. In the first place, his staff knew that David was doing something, but not what. In the second, they were expected to contribute to subjects on which they either had little experience or no direct involvement. So despite David's efforts, he was contributing to his team's stress.

Liz's foresight reduces stress

The only time that Liz Cole's staff were under pressure, was when a large number of people booked into the hotel at the same time, for instance delegates to a conference. At these times Liz ensured that there were sufficient staff on duty to cope with the extra work load. She also made sure that each member of her staff took adequate breaks during the working day and that no one did more overtime than was absolutely necessary.

As a result of her management, none of Liz's staff felt under undue pressure or showed any signs of stress. If they did, then she would know that it was due to a domestic problem and would take the appropriate action.

SUMMARY

Good stress management
- Be aware of changes in behaviour of the staff and take appropriate action, eg a counselling interview.
- Encourage communication.
- Make sure that everyone is aware of the acceptable work standards.
- Encourage appropriate involvement by the staff.
- Do not overload the staff with work but make sure that everyone has sufficient to keep them occupied.
- Ensure that everybody takes proper coffee, lunch and tea breaks away from the work place.
- Never show that you are under stress.
- Discourage too much overtime.

Bad stress management
- Being unaware or ignoring behavourial changes.
- Operating a 'closed door' policy.
- 'Dumping' rather than delegating.
- Making sure that your staff do not leave their work place during the working day.
- Keeping all information to yourself.
- Being inflexible with 'rules and regulations'.

DISCUSSION POINTS

1. How involved should you become with your staff's personal and domestic problems?

2. What can you do to lessen the possibility of stress within your working environment?

3. Which of the following are likely to be signs of impending stress:
   - Increased absenteeism.
   - Being late for work every Monday.
   - Unwillingness to participate in outside activities organised by the team.
   - More introverted behaviour.
   - Showing aggression at the slightest mishap.
   - Spending more time in the toilet.
   - Working late more often than usual.
   - Joking about problems and complaints.

14
Looking to the Future

MANAGEMENT AS A SEPARATE SKILL

I have been asked to conclude by gazing into my crystal ball and making some predictions about management in the future.

Having read the book thus far, you will have come to realise that there is more to being a good and effective manager than meets the eye. It is not simply an extension to 'the job' but requires specific techniques to be learned and practised.

TRAINING

Many large organisations, particularly in the retail industry, operate comprehensive management training schemes. In general these are excellent but, of course, confined only to employees of the companies concerned. I would hope that in the not too distant future, all potential managers will be required to undergo a thorough training in the necessary skills and techniques before being let loose on their unsuspecting staff. Ideally, this will lead to a nationally accepted qualification that all managers must possess before being appointed. After all, would you let yourself be examined by an unqualified doctor, or employ an unqualified electrician to rewire your house?

At present there are a limited number of courses leading to a management qualification, of which the MBA (Master of Business Administration) is the highest. However, these courses pay scant reference to the management of the most important resource—people. As a result, graduates tend to be 'academic' managers. The ideal training would be based on the 'sandwich course' principle, part of the time being spent in the classroom and part working in companies to gain practical experience. Perhaps one day management will be recognised as a profession alongside accountancy, law and medicine.

WOMEN MANAGERS

The discussion regarding the lack of women in management has been going on for many years. Being an advocate of equal opportunities, I would like to see more women managers. However, the situation will only change when attitudes change too. Matters are not helped by those organisations that run courses and seminars called 'Women in Management' and 'Assertiveness for Women'. These only serve to highlight a difference which does not really exist. The skills required by male and female managers are identical, and hopefully in the future they will be treated as such.

THE IMPACT OF TECHNOLOGY

With the rapid increases in information technology and electronic communication, it is highly likely that more people will work from home. How will these people be managed? Sales managers have been faced with a similar problem for many years. They try to solve it by having regular team meetings, accompanying their staff on field visits and keeping in touch by telephone. All of these techniques except the field visit can be used by the managers of these 'out workers'. However, the main difficulty will be preventing demotivation.

It is also quite probable that more people will become self employed, hiring their services to companies for a fixed period of time. Contract computer programmers operate in a similar way at present. How can you manage someone who is virtually their own boss? In these circumstances it may well be that the role of the first line manager will have to change to that of a co-ordinator.

It is recognised, if not always accepted, that the standards of British managers fall well below those of the other major industrial countries. One of the reasons given is that overseas managers are better paid than those in Britain. This may well be true but the real reasons are inadequate training, traditional methods of promotion and outdated social attitudes.

MANAGEMENT AS A PROFESSION

So does management have a future? I am confident that it does. However, radical changes are necessary. It will be vital to have one regulatory body, responsible for all managers in the United Kingdom. Law has the Law Society, medicine the British Medical Authority, so why not a British Management Council?

My predictions for the future are:

- Managers will be recognised as requiring specific skills and techniques in order to be effective.

- All potential managers will receive adequate training before they are appointed with special attention being paid to human management skills.

- Management will become a recognised profession with one regulatory body.

- Men and women will be treated equally in management opportunities.

- The role of the manager will change to adapt to different working methods.

You are the future of management. If you want changes it will be up to you to bring them about. Your thoughts and actions will determine future trends and attitudes.

Thank you for reading this book; I hope you have found it useful. May I take this opportunity to wish you every success in your management career.

Appendix A
Discussion points: suggested solutions

There can never be definitive answers to problems involving people, so these are only suggestions for handling the problems posed at the end of each chapter.

Chapter 1 (see page 19)

2. Arrange an informal interview with Bill Atkinson to discover the extent of his knowledge and experience. Discuss how these can be best used to help you and the team. Make a few early decisions which affect your staff and then involve them as quickly as possible. If it is appropriate, appoint Bill as your unofficial deputy.

Chapter 3 (see pages 35-36)

2(a) 'You are concerned that you may not be able to take your holiday.'
2(b) 'You feel upset.'
2(c) 'The increasing amount of traffic is making you feel frustrated.'

Chapter 4 (see page 46)

4. See Chapter 6 – Approaching Retirement (page 63).

Chapter 5 (see page 60)

3. Discuss the situation with your team explaining the reason. Arrange for a rota, including yourself, to clean the office and agree to keep the office as tidy as possible during the day.

Chapter 6 (see page 74)

2. Tell – Emergencies eg fire.
    Sell – Passing on directives from above.
    Test – Where you have more experience of the problem than your team.
    Consult – When your staff have some experience of similar situations.

Join – When members of your team are likely to have more experience of the problem than you.

Delegate – Where the decision will only affect your staff.

Chapter 7 (see page 80)
2. Only when you have carefully considered all the options and there is no alternative.

Chapter 8 (see pages 90-91)
2. David Wilson needs to explain to Wally Dickson the consequences of not receiving his visit reports in writing. He should stop accepting verbal reports and complete his weekly report on Fridays omitting Wally's reports if they are not available.
3. Brian needs to prepare an agenda for the monthly meetings, dealing first with those points on which he has already made a decision. This would be followed by the points on which he wants contributions from the group. The Managers must put forward their suggestions, backed up by as many facts and figures as possible in anticipation of Brian's 'logical' response.

Chapter 9 (see page 102)
3. Explain to your manager that you have scheduled your time for that day. If he insists, ask him to prioritise your tasks to enable the report to be prepared. Tell him that given more notice you would be able to prepare a more accurate, detailed report.

Chapter 10 (see page 104)
The Nine Dots (see page 104)

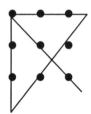

Who told you to stay within the square?

Ambulance and sheep (see page 105)

Stop the ambulance and ask the shepherd to turn the flock around and drive them past the stationary ambulance.

Golf ball in the bag (see page 105)
   Set light to the paper bag.

The cake (see page 110)

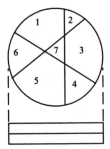

Three vertical cuts and a horizontal one through the side.

The farmer's field (see page 110)

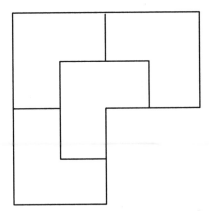

Chapter 11 (see page 123)

1. The corner position would be the most suitable for all types of interview. If you know the interviewee well you can try the open position for counselling.
3. In each case, remain silent and let the person vent their feelings, then respond as follows:
   (a) You feel upset because...
   (b) You feel angry because...
   (c) You feel annoyed because...

Chapter 12 (see page 129)

1. Arthur should firstly have questioned his director about the decision, pointing out the negative effect it would have on his salesmen. If the position remains the same he should sell the situation to his staff, explaining the reasons.
2. David Wilson should have responded to Tony Rawlins remark about moving offices by asking him to verify the matter and taking no further action.

Chapter 13 (see page 138)

1. Only as much as it may affect the work and/or the team.
2. – regular, open communication,
   – getting the team involved in decisions,
   – training and delegation,
   – preventing excessive work loads,
3. All of them.

Who's Who

Chapter 1
Peter F Drucker – US management guru
Casey Stengel – US baseball player & manager
Laurence J Peter – Canadian author & educator

Chapter 2
Robert Frost – US poet
HRH Prince Philip – Duke of Edinburgh

Chapter 3
Sidney J Harris – US scientist
James Thurber – US humourist

Chapter 4
William James – US philosopher
Harriet Beecher Stowe – US authoress (*Uncle Tom's Cabin*)

Chapter 5
T H White – US sociologist
Walter Lippman – US journalist
J C Penny – US retailing magnate
John Bunyan – British theologian

Chapter 6
Robert Townsend – former chairman of Avis Car Rentals
Sir Archibald Wavell – World War Two military leader

Chapter 7
Fletcher Knebel – US writer
E J Thomas – US psychologist

Chapter 8
Henry Ford – US industrialist and car manufacturer
Poul Anderson – US science fiction writer

Chapter 9
Carl T Rowan – US columnist

Chapter 10
Edmund Burke – British 18th century politician
Alfred P Sloane – former chairman of General Motors
William T Brady – US impresario
Edward de Bono – writer and lecturer on thinking skills

Chapter 11
Mark Twain – US author
Oscar Wilde – Irish writer and wit

Chapter 12
Sir John Harvey Jones – former chairman of ICI
D L Foster – US lawyer and writer

Chapter 13
Dr Vernon Coleman – British lecturer and writer on stress

Glossary

Agenda List of topics to be discussed at a meeting.

Appraisal Review of an employee's performance with his/her immediate manager.

Behaviour Way in which people react in given situations.

Body language Gestures and postures which convey the hidden message behind verbal communication.

Brainstorm Method of involving a group of people in solving problems.

Communication The exchange of ideas and information between groups or individuals to achieve a mutual understanding.

Core problem The real personal problem, hidden behind a presenting problem.

Correction A more appropriate term for discipline.

Counselling An interviewing technique for revealing the core problem and helping the owner of the problem to reach a solution.

Decision Choices to be made between two or more options.

Delegate To hand over a task to another person together with the authority and responsibility.

Evaluate To review the result of a decision or solution.

Force field analysis A method of solving problems where the objective is to move the status quo.

Grievance A dispute between two or more people.

Hygiene factor An area within a company which, when improved, will not necessarily motivate employees, eg salary, working conditions.

Incentive A reward offered for performing certain tasks or actions.

Innovation Making changes, introducing new ideas, methods or practices.

Interview A formal conversation between two people to achieve a specific objective.

Jargon Language of technical or special words. A verbal shorthand.

Lateral thinking Opposite of horizontal or logical thinking. Creative thinking.

Leadership styles Different methods of leading or managing, dependent upon the situation and the people involved.

Manager One who leads, motivates and develops others to achieve an agreed objective.

Mentor An experienced and trusted person assigned to help less experienced people.

Mind mapping A method of putting ideas on paper in a random manner as opposed to a list.

Motivate To offer the appropriate incentives to satisfy people's needs in order to persuade them to undertake tasks to behave in a required manner.

Objectives Targets or goals which can be quantified.

People The most important, valuable and costly resource of any company or organisation.

Problems Questions or situations which require a solution.

Quality circles Groups of people from a department in a company, whose purpose is to solve departmental problems.

Recognition A means of motivating people.

Reflective technique A listening skill.

Resources What a manager has to manage, eg people, space and time.

Risk analysis A means of assisting the decision-making process.

Stress A mental state brought about by excessive pressure of events both at work and at home.

Team A group of people working together to achieve a specific objective.

Time management Planning to use time in the most effective manner.

Training Plan A chart illustrating who needs training and in what areas.

Zones The space around each individual, viz intimate, personal, social and public.

Further Reading

GENERAL

How To Be An.Even Better Manager, Michael Armstrong (Kogan Page 1988)

How to Know Your Rights at Work, Robert Spicer (How To Books, 2nd edition 1995)

EMS: Managing People, John Scott & Arthur Rochester (Sphere/BIM 1984)

The Management Handbook, Arthur Young (Sphere 1986)

First Time Manager, Joan Iaconetti & Patrick O'Hara (MacMillan 1985)

COMMUNICATION

Effective Employee Communication, Michael Bland & Peter Jackson (Kogan Page)

Body Language, Allan Pease (Sheldon Press 1981)

Understanding Body Language, Jane Lyle (Hamlyn 1989)

How to Communicate at Work, Ann Dobson (How To Books, 1994)

How to Master Business English, Michael Bennie (How To Books, 2nd edition 1994)

How to Master Public Speaking, Anne Nicholls (How To Books, 3rd edition 1995)

How to Publish a Newsletter, Graham Jones (How To Books, 2nd edition 1995)

How to Write a Report, John Bowden (How To Books, 2nd edition 1994)

FINANCE

Accounting & Finance For Business Students, Mike Bendry, Roger Hussey and Colston West (DP Publications 1989)

How to Manage Budgets & Cash Flows, Peter Taylor (How To Books, 1994)

How to Understand Finance at Work (How To Books, 1994)

INNOVATION

Master Thinker's Handbook, Edward de Bono (Penguin 1985)

PROBLEMS

How to Counsel People at Work, John Humphries (How To Books 1995)

Solving People Problems, Peter Honey (McGraw Hill 1980)

Effective Problem Solving, Dave Francis (Routledge 1990)

RECRUITMENT

How To Employ and Manage Staff, Wendy Wyatt (How To Books, 2nd edition 1995)

SELF MANAGEMENT

A Manager's Guide to Self Development, Pedler, Burgoyne & Boydell (McGraw Hill 1978)

STRESS

Stress Management Techniques, Dr Vernon Coleman (Mercury Business Books 1988)

Managing Pressure At Work, Helen Froggatt & Paul Stamp (BBC 1987)

TEAMS & LEADERSHIP

How to Conduct Staff Appraisals, Nigel Hunt (How To Books, 2nd edition 1994)

Not Bosses But Leaders, John Adair (Kogan Page 1978)

Teamwork, Vincent Nolan (Sphere 1987)

TIME

Manage Your Time, Sally Garret (Fontana 1985)

Getting Things Done, Roger Black (Michael Joseph 1987)

Index

153

How to Conduct Staff Appraisals
Nigel Hunt

Managers and organisations neglect staff appraisal at their peril today. But what exactly is staff appraisal? Why is it now so vital, and what are the benefits? Should senior as well as junior staff undergo appraisal, and how could this be done? This book, now in a new edition, sets out a basic framework which every manager can use or adapt, whether in business and industry, transport, education, health and public services. 'Informative...Points for discussion and case studies are prominent throughout... the case studies are highly relevant and good.' *Progress (NEBS Management Association Journal)*. Nigel Hunt is a consultant in occupational testing, selection, appraisal, vocational assessment, and management development. He is a Graduate Member of the British Psychological Society, and Associate Member of the Institute of Personnel & Development.
154pp illus. 1 85703 1172. 2nd edition.

How to Employ & Manage Staff
Wendy Wyatt

This easy to use handbook will help all managers and supervisors whose work involves them in recruiting and managing staff. Ideal for quick reference, it provides a ready-made framework of modern employment practice from recruitment onwards. It provides a clear account of how to apply the health & safety at work regulations, how to handle record-keeping, staff development, grievance and disciplinary procedures, maternity and sick leave and similar matters for the benefit of the organisation and its employees. The book includes a useful summary of current employment legislation and is complete with a range of model forms, letters, notices and similar documents. Wendy Wyatt GradIPD is a Personnel Management and Employment Consultant; her other books include *Recruiting Success* and *Jobhunt*, and she has contributed regularly to the press on employment matters.
128pp illus. 1 85703 167 9. 2nd edition.

How to Know Your Rights at Work
Robert Spicer MA

Written in clear English, this easy-to-follow handbook sets out everyone's rights at work whether in an office, shop, factory or other setting. Frequent use is made of recent court cases to illustrate the text. 'Justifiably described as a practical guide to employment law. It is clearly written in language readily understood by the layman... The text has been well laid out and sections are clearly signposted... The extensive use of case study material is interesting and helpful .. interesting enough in its own right to be read from cover to cover.' *Careers Officer journal*. 'Sets out in simple English everything an employee can expect in today's working environment.' *Kent Evening Post*. 'All in all a welcome addition to the libraries of advice-giving agencies, trade unions and employers alike.' *Frontline*. 'A very useful basic guide.' *Newscheck/Careers Service Bulletin*. Robert Spicer MA(Cantab) is a practising barrister, legal editor and author who specialises in employment law.
141pp. 1 85703 172 5. 2nd edition.

How to Master Business English
Michael Bennie

Are you communicating effectively? Do your business documents achieve the results
you want? Or are they too often ignored or misunderstood? Good communication is the
key to success in any business. Whether you are trying to sell a product, answer a query
or complaint, or persuade colleagues, the way you express yourself is often as important
as what you say. With lots of examples, checklists and questionnaires to help you, this
book will speed you on your way, 'An excellent book – not in the least dull ...
Altogether most useful for anyone seeking to improve their communication skills.' *IPS
Journal.* 'Gives guidance on writing styles for every situation... steers the reader
through the principles and techniques of effective letter-writing and document-
planning.' *First Voice.* 'Useful chapters on grammar, punctuation and spelling.
Frequent questionnaires and checklists enable the reader to check progress.' *Focus
(Society of Business Teachers).* 'The language and style is easy to follow... Excellent
value for money.' *Spoken English.*
208pp illus. 1 845703 129 6. 2nd edition.

How to Master Public Speaking
Anne Nicholls

Speaking well in public is one of the most useful skills any of us can acquire. People who
can often become leaders in their business, profession or community, and the envy of
their friends and colleagues. Whether you are a nervous novice or a practised pro, this
step-by-step handbook tells you everything you need to know to master this highly
prized communication skill. Contents: Preface, being a skilled communicator,
preparation, researching your audience, preparing a speech, finding a voice, body
language and non-verbal communication, dealing with nerves, audiovisual aids, the
physical environment, putting it all together on the day, audience feedback, dealing
with the media, glossary, further reading, useful contacts, index. Anne Hulbert Nicholls
BA(Hons) PGCE was a Lecturer in Communications and Journalism in a College of
Education for 14 years and ran courses in Presentation Skills and Effective Speaking for
local business people. She now runs seminars and conferences for a publishing
company and writes articles for a number of national magazines and newspapers. Her
articles appear regularly in *Living* magazine. She has also worked in Public Relations
and for BBC Radio.
160pp illus. 1 85703 149 0. 3rd edition.

How to Write a Report
John Bowden

Communicating effectively on paper is an essential skill for today's business or professional person. Good report-writing is a highly effective means of achieving a wide range of objectives, for example in managing an organisation, dealing with staffing, sales and marketing, production, computer operations, financial planning and reporting, feasibility studies and business innovation. Written by an experienced manager and staff trainer, this well-presented handbook provides a very clear step-by-step framework for every individual, whether dealing with professional colleagues, customers, clients, suppliers or junior or senior staff. Contents: Preparation and planning. Collecting and handling information. Writing the report: principles and techniques. Improving your thinking. Improving presentation. Achieving a good writing style. Making effective use of English. How to choose and use illustrations. Choosing paper, covers and binding. Appendices (examples, techniques, checklists), glossary, index. John Bowden BSc(Econ) MSc studied at the London School of Economics. He has long experience both as a professional manager in industry, and as a Senior Lecturer running courses in accountancy, auditing, and effective communication, up to senior management level.
160pp illus. 091 5. 2nd edition.

How to Pass That Interview
Judith Johnstone

Everyone knows how to shine at interview — or do they? When every candidate becomes the perfect clone of the one before, you have to have that extra 'something' to raise your chances above the rest. Using a systematic and practical approach, this new How To book takes you step-by-step through the essential pre-interview groundwork, the interview encounter itself, and what you can learn from the experience afterwards. The book contains sample pre- and post-interview correspondence, and is complete with a guide to further reading, glossary of terms, and index. 'This is from the first class How To Books stable.' *Escape Committee Newsletter.* 'Offers a fresh approach to a well documented subject.' *Newscheck/Careers Service Bulletin.* 'A complete step-by-step guide.' *The Association of Business Executives.* Judith Johnstone has written extensively on employment-related subjects. A Graduate of the Institute of Personnel & Development, she has been an instructor in Business Studies and adult literacy tutor, and has long experience of helping people at work.
128pp illus. 1 85703 118 0. 2nd edition.

How to Keep Business Accounts
Peter Taylor

A new revised edition of an easy-to-understand handbook for all business owners and managers. 'Will help you sort out the best way to carry out double entry book-keeping, as well as providing a clear step-by-step guide to accounting procedures.' *Mind Your Own Business.* 'Progresses through the steps to be taken to maintain an effective double entry book-keeping system with the minimum of bother.' *The Accounting Technician.* 'Compulsory reading.' *Manager, National Westminster Bank (Midlands).* Peter Taylor is a Fellow of the Institute of Chartered Accountants, and of the Chartered Association of Certified Accountants. He has many years' practical experience of advising small businesses.
176pp illus. 85703 111 3. 3rd edition.

How to Master Book-Keeping
Peter Marshall

Book-keeping can seem a confusing subject for people coming to it for the first time. This very clear book will be welcomed by everyone wanting a really user-friendly guide to recording business transactions step-by-step. Illustrated at every stage with specimen entries, the book will also be an ideal companion for students taking LCCI, RSA, BTEC, accountancy technician and similar courses at schools, colleges or training centres. Typical business transactions are used to illustrate all the essential theory, practice and skills required to be effective in a real business setting. Contents: Preface, introduction, theory of double entry, day books, cash book, bank reconciliation, petty cash book, journal, postage book, the ledger, discounts, control accounts, trial balance, accruals and prepayments, revenue accounts, the balance sheet, manufacturing accounts, depreciation, bad and doubtful debts, partnership and accounts, amalgamation of sole proprietorships into a partnership, limited companies, 'going limited', club accounts, asset disposals, correction of errors, VAT accounts, incomplete records, interpretation of accounts, wages, stock records. Peter Marshall BSc(Econ) BA(Hons) FRSA FSBT MBIM has been Tutor in Education at the University of Lancaster and Director of Studies at the Careers College, Cardiff. He has contributed regularly to *FOCUS on Business Education.*
176pp illus. 1 85703 065 6. 2nd edition.

How to Raise Business Finance
Peter Ibbetson

Every business needs to raise money from time to time. It may be for start-up capital, to cover a difficult cash flow, to invest in research and development, to finance new equipment, premises, or exports, or to restructure the business as a whole. Written by a professional banker, this highly readable book explains what finance costs, what base rates and APR mean, how fixed interest loans work. It discusses where cash can be found in a business, for example from existing debtors/creditors, as well as outside lenders. It considers the importance of the balance sheet, track record, gearing, overheads, project viability, and the importance of cash flow forecasting (explaining why this may differ markedly from profit forecasts). Equity financing and management buyouts are explained too, and the role of financial institutions and government sources summarised. Whole chapters are devoted to special forms of finance such as leasing, factoring, contract hire, and finance for exporters, backed up with pages of key references, contacts and addresses, and a helpful glossary of financial and banking terms. 'Gives the right amount of information.' *Association of British Chambers of Commerce*. 'A lucid account of the steps by which a small businessman can substantially strengthen his case.' *The Financial Times*. Peter Ibbetson is an Associate of the Chartered Institute of Bankers, and an author and broadcaster on banking matters. *160pp illus. 07463 0338 6.*

How to Invest in Stocks and Shares
Dr John White

This book has been specially prepared to help and guide those with a substantial sum to invest (often more than £50,000) and who are considering investing all or part of this sum in quoted securities. Often such investors have such a sum as a result of a recent inheritance, for example when the house of a deceased parent has been sold. This new book recognises that such investors are not normally interested in suspect get-rich-quick schemes, but rather in a practical and level-headed approach in which longterm objectives are important. This book therefore provides a complete step-by-step framework to share selection and dealing, and portfolio management, against a background of longer term trends. Dr John White, an Oxford graduate, is himself an experienced investor and adviser to an investment company. He has a professional background in computers and has produced a range of software for chart analysis. *192pp illus. 1 85703 112 1. 2nd edition.*

How to Start a Business from Home
Graham Jones

Most people have dreamed of starting their own business from home at some time or
other; but how do you begin? What special skills do you need? This great value-for-
money paperback has the answers, showing how you can profit from your own talents
and experience, and start turning spare time into cash from the comfort of your own
home. *How to Start a Business From Home* contains a wealth of ideas, projects, tips,
facts, checklists and quick-reference information for everyone — whether in between
jobs, taking early retirement, or students and others with time to invest. Packed with
information on everything from choosing a good business idea and starting up to
advertising, book-keeping and dealing with professionals, this book is essential reading
for every budding entrepreneur. 'Full of ideas and advice.' *The Daily Mirror*. Graham
Jones BSc(Hons) is an editor, journalist and lecturer specialising in practical business
subjects. His other books include *Fit to Manage* and *The Business of Freelancing*.
176pp, 1 85703 126 1. 3rd edition.

How to Do Your Own Advertising
Michael Bennie

'Entrepreneurs and small businesses are flooding the market with new products and
services; the only way to beat the competition is successful selling — and that means
advertising.' But what can you afford? This book is for anyone who needs — or wants
— to advertise effectively, but does not want to pay agency rates. It will also be useful to
those who simply want to know what is involved in advertising, whether as students,
business people or interested laymen. What are the secrets of putting together effective
ads? Even the basic design can be done by someone with a little imagination and
creativity. This book shows you step-by-step how to assemble a simple, straightforward,
yet highly successful ad or brochure with the minimum of outside help. Every step is
clearly explained with the beginner in mind. There are numerous illustrations, lots of
examples of actual ads, a variety of case studies to show the principles in practice and
the aim throughout is to make advertising easy and enjoyable. Complete with
questionnaires and checklists to help you check your progress. Michael Bennie has had
many years' professional experience as a Sales Manager with a number of international
companies, covering all aspects of sales and copywriting. He is now a freelance
copywriter and advertising consultant, and Director of Studies at the Copywriting
School.
176pp illus. 0 7463 0579 6.